ABOUT THE AUTHOR

Moustafa Gadalla was born in Cairo, Egypt in 1944. He graduated from Cairo University with a Bachelor of Science in civil engineering in 1967. He immigrated to the U.S.A. in 1971 to practice engineering as a licensed professional engineer and land surveyor. He is an independent Egyptologist who spent most of his adult life studying and researching scores of books about Egyptian texts, history, traditions, knowledge, Egypt's worldwide influence, etc.

He is the author of seven internationally-acclaimed books. He is the chairman of the Tehuti Research Foundation, an international, U.S.-based, non-profit organization, dedicated to Ancient Egyptian studies. He spends a part of every year visiting and studying sites of antiquities.

OTHER BOOKS BY THE AUTHOR

Historical Deception
The Untold Story of Ancient Egypt (2nd Ed.)
ISBN: 0-9652509-2-X (pbk.), 352 pages, US$19.95

Egyptian Harmony: The Visual Music
ISBN: 0-9652509-8-9 (pbk.), 160 pages, US$11.95

Pyramid Handbook
ISBN: 0-9652509-4-6 (pbk.), 192 pages, US$11.95

Exiled Egyptians: The Heart of Africa
ISBN: 0-9652509-6-2 (pbk.), 352 pages, US$19.95

Egypt: A Practical Guide
ISBN: 0-9652509-3-0 (pbk.), 256 pages, US$8.50

Tut-Ankh-Amen: The Living Image of the Lord
ISBN: 0-9652509-9-7 (pbk.), 144 pages, US$9.50

Testimonials of the First Edition

The Independent Review - 1/98 - Armidale, Australia
...[Gadalla's] grasp of Egyptian cosmology is awesome, he explains how the Neteru were not Gods or Goddesses but principles...From this basis he is able to reconstruct the real religion of Egypt, both as esotericism and as general practices. Far from being a primitive, polytheistic form, we have the highest expression of monotheistic mysticism...

Amazon.com Online Bookstore (http://www.amazon.com)
Occult and Metaphysics Editor's Recommended Book, 01/15/98:
Moustafa Gadalla's controversial Egyptian Cosmology: The Absolute Harmony shatters the centuries-old view of Egyptian deities (Neteru) as mythical figures, and instead proposes that the Neteru are not gods, but representations of different aspects of one supreme being. Gadalla seeks to rectify these and other errors that have been perpetuated by scholars since the time of the ancient Greeks. Egyptian Cosmology highlights the intelligence of this ancient civilization whose beliefs are reflected in 20th-century concepts such as the big bang theory....

Internet Bookwatch - Oct 1997 - Wisconsin, USA
Moustafa Gadalla's Egyptian Cosmology: The Absolute Harmony describes, showcases in reader-friendly fashion, the remarkably advanced concepts embodied within ancient Egyptian metaphysics. Egyptian concepts which served as the source of Western and Eastern metaphysics. Readers will discover that Egyptian cosmology is coherent, comprehensive, consistent, logical, analytical, and rational. From the casual reader to the serious student of metaphysics, Egyptian Cosmology is nothing short of fascinating as it surveys the applicability of Egyptian concepts to our modern understandings of the nature of the universe, creation, science, and philosophy. Egyptian Cosmology is an outstanding contribution to metaphysical studies.

Book Production by: Moustafa Gadalla and Faith Cross
Book Cover Artwork by: K&D Design, North East, PA, USA

Egyptian Cosmology

The Animated Universe

Second Edition, Revised

Moustafa Gadalla
Maa Kheru (True of Voice)

Tehuti Research Foundation
International Head Office: Greensboro, NC, U.S.A.

Egyptian Cosmology
The Animated Universe
by Moustafa Gadalla

Published by:
Tehuti Research Foundation
P.O. Box 39406
Greensboro, NC   27438-9406, U.S.A.

This book is a revised and enhanced edition of the originally titled *Egyptian Cosmology: The Absolute Harmony,* by Moustafa Gadalla. The name was changed to better reflect the expanded content of the book.

Publisher's Cataloging in Publication Data
(Provided by Quality Books, Inc.)

Gadalla, Moustafa, 1944-
   Egyptian cosmology : the animated universe / Moustafa Gadalla. -- 2nd ed., rev.
   p. cm.
   Includes bibliographical references and index.
   Preassigned LCCN: 2001 130122
   ISBN: 0-9652509-3-8
   Originally published as: Egyptian cosmology : the absolute harmony.

   1. Cosmology, Egyptian. 2. Egypt--Religion.
3. Egypt--Civilization. 4. Occultism--Egypt. 5. Science--Egypt--History. I. Title.

BL2443.G33 2001   299'.31
                                              QBI01-200011

Manufactured in the United States of America
Published 2001

Table of Contents

Part I
The Egyptian Way

Part II
The Creation Numerical Codes

Part ▮▮▮
The Energy Matrix

Part ▌▌▌▌
The Universal Replica

Part ▌▌▌
Social Harmony

Part **III**
The Earthly Voyage

Part ▌▌▌▌
Going Home

Part ▌▌▌▌
A New Octave

Dedicated to
The Baladi People of Egypt,
The Bearers of Their Ancestral Torch
...The Survivors

Playing with an Egg and a Stone

Preface

Almost all Egyptologists interpreted, and continue to interpret, the Ancient Egyptian writings and other modes of expression (art, architecture, ...etc.) without trying to understand the thoughts and beliefs expressed in them. Their explanations continue to be shallow, which reflects their pre-conceived notions of the Ancient Egyptians as being primitive and inferior to the *modern Western world*.

About a half-century ago, Alexandre Piankoff summed up the deteriorated status of Egyptology in the following statements from his book, *The Tomb of Ramses VI*, 1954:

> *For the early Egyptologists this religion was highly mysterious and mystical. They saw it with eyes of a Father Kircher. Then came a sudden reaction: scholars lost all interest in the religion as such and viewed the religious texts merely as source material for their philological-historical research. Under the sway of Higher Criticism, the texts were decomposed and their genesis eagerly studied...The intrinsic value of religious composition and thought was systematically ignored and consequently temporarily lost. Egyptian scholars since Champollion saw in the oldest religious lore of humanity mainly a collection of distorted historical data out of which he endeavored all his life to reconstruct the history of ancient Egypt.*

I share with Piankoff his assessment of the present and future state of Egyptology.

> *We are now at the beginning of a new era, one in which the necessity of fusion, of a synthesis of the mystical and the historical approach, is being felt. Moreover, with the appearance of psychoanalytic studies, the Egyptian religious symbols have suddenly acquired a new, an intimate meaning.*
> *At the present stage, an attempt to render the pregnant*

religious writings of Egypt in a modern language still remains a bold undertaking; yet it is worth while to try.

Many conflicting sides, who use Ancient Egypt to promote each's own agenda, insist that the ancient religion and traditions have died. The truth is that they never died, and they continue to survive within the silent majority — the Baladi people of Egypt. Even though the loud minority — the Afrangi (meaning *foreign-like*) Egyptians — dominate the spotlight, the Baladi Egyptians continue to maintain their ancestor traditions.

I sincerely hope that this book will prompt many people (not just archeologists and academicians) to listen and learn from the treasure of knowledge imbedded in the Baladi Egyptian traditions. We then must re-read and re-examine the Ancient Egyptian writings with an open mind. This is an investment in our own future, for Egypt is the *ancient future*, where as per Hermetic Texts — Asleptus III (25),

"...the whole cosmos dwells in Egypt as in its sanctuary..."

Moustafa Gadalla

Standards and Terminology

1 - You may find a variety in writing the same Ancient Egyptian term such as **Amen/Amon/Amun.** The reason is, that the vowels you see in translated Egyptian texts are an approximation of sound that are used by Egyptologists to help them pronounce the Ancient Egyptian terms/words.

2 - The Ancient Egyptian word, **neter**, and its feminine form **netert**, have been wrongly, and possibly intentionally, translated to *god* and *goddess*, by almost all academicians.
Neteru (plural of **neter/netert**) are the divine principles and functions of the One Supreme God.

3 - When referring to the names of cities, Pharaohs, **neteru**, etc., if the commonly used Greek name is different than the true Egyptian name, we will show the correct Egyptian name **(in this font)** followed by the common, but arbitrary Greek rendering between parentheses.

4 - The term *Baladi* will be used throughout this book to denote the present silent majority of Egyptians that adhere to the Ancient Egyptian traditions, with a thin exterior layer of islam. The christian population of Egypt is an ethnic minority that came as refugees, from Judaea and Syria to the Ptolemaic/Roman-ruled Alexandria. Now, 2,000 years later, they are easily distinguishable in looks and mannerisms from the majority of native Egyptians. [See *Exiled Egyptians: The Heart of Africa*, by same author, and our website (URL on last page), for detailed information.]

5 - There were/are no Ancient Egyptian writings/texts that were categorized by the Egyptians themselves as "religious", "funerary", "sacred", ...etc. Western academia gave the Ancient Egyptian texts arbitrary names, such as the "Book of This", and the "Book of That", "divisions", "utterances", "spells", ...etc. Western academia even decided that a certain "Book" had a "Theban version" or "this or that time period version". After believing their own dogmatic creation, academia accused the Ancient Egyptians of making mistakes and missing portions of their writing?!!

For ease of reference, we will mention the common but arbitrary Western academic categorization of Ancient Egyptian texts, even though the Ancient Egyptians themselves never did.

6 - Throughout this book, the fonting of quotations varies depending on the source of quotation. There are generally two types of fonting:

Δ *This font is used to refer to Ancient Egyptian sources.*

Δ *This font is to refer to quotes from other sources.*

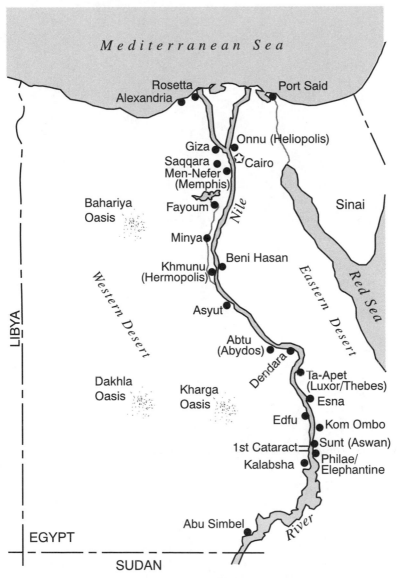

N

0   100   200 miles

0   150   300 km

Mediterranean Sea

Rosetta
Alexandria

Port Said

Onnu (Heliopolis)

Giza
Saqqara
Men-Nefer
(Memphis)

Cairo

Nile

Sinai

Bahariya
Oasis

Fayoum

Red Sea

Minya

Khmunu
(Hermopolis)

Beni Hasan

Western Desert

Asyut

Eastern Desert

Abtu
(Abydos)

Dendara

Ta-Apet
(Luxor/Thebes)

Dakhla
Oasis

Kharga
Oasis

Esna

Edfu

Kom Ombo

Sunt (Aswan)

1st Cataract

Philae/
Elephantine

Kalabsha

Abu Simbel

River

LIBYA

EGYPT

SUDAN

Part

I

The Egyptian Way

Chapter 1

The Most Religious

Cosmic Consciousness

The Greek historian Herodotus (500 BCE) stated:

*Of all the nations of the world, the Egyptians are the happi-
est, healthiest and most religious.*

The excellent condition of the Egyptians was attributed
to their application of metaphysical realities in their daily
life — in other words — total cosmic consciousness.

The scenes of daily activities, found inside Egyptian
tombs, show a strong perpetual correlation between the earth
and heavens. The scenes provide graphical representation
of all manner of activities: hunting, fishing, agriculture, law
courts, and all kinds of arts and crafts. Portraying these
daily activities, in the presence of the **neteru** (gods) or with
their assistance, signifies their cosmic correspondence.

This perpetual correlation — cosmic consciousness —
was echoed in *Asleptus III (25)* of the *Hermetic Texts*:

*"...in Egypt all the operations of the powers which rule and
work in heaven have been transferred to earth below...it
should rather be said that the whole cosmos dwells in
[Egypt] as in its sanctuary..."*

Every action, no matter how mundane, was in some sense a cosmic correspondence act: plowing, sowing, reaping, brewing, the size of a beer mug, the shape of a pyramid, building ships, waging wars, playing games — all were viewed as earthly symbols for divine activities.

In Egypt, what we now call religion, was so widely acknowledged that it did not even need a name. For them, there was no perceived difference between sacred and mundane. All their knowledge that was based on cosmic consciousness was embedded into their daily practices, which became traditions.

Foreign visitors to Egypt, who are unfamiliar with the cosmic depth of the natives' traditions, are unwise to hastily label the Ancient and Baladi Egyptians as "superstitious".

We do many things in life, such as operating the computer, without most of us knowing how it works. This does not invalidate our computer use as being unscientific. Likewise, the Ancient and Baladi Egyptians' practices should not be dismissed because not everyone knows the scientific basis for that perpetual cosmic action.

In any society, only a relatively few specialized people know the scientific basis for how/why things work in certain ways.

True Monotheism

The Ancient Egyptians believed in One God who was self-produced, self-existent, immortal, invisible, eternal, omniscient, almighty, etc. This One God was never represented. It is the functions and attributes of his domain that were represented. These attributes were called the **neteru** (pronounced *net-er-u,* singular: **neter** in the masculine form and **netert** in the feminine form). The term, *gods,* is a misrepresentation of the Egyptian term, **neteru.**

One can only define "God" through the multitude of "his" attributes/qualities/powers/actions. This is the only logical way, because if we refer to, say, a person as Mr. X, it means nothing to us. However, once we describe his attributes and qualities, we then begin to know him. A person who is an engineer, a father, a husband, ... etc. does not have poly-personalities, but rather a mono-personality with multiple functions/attributes. For the Ancient and Baladi Egyptians, the concept of God is similar.

The part-Egyptian Akhenaton failed to understand/respect the Egyptian rationale, and butchered the multiple attributes of God in choosing one attribute — **Aton.** [More about him in *Historical Deception: The Untold Story of Ancient Egypt,* by same author.]

Judaism, Christianity, and Islam assume that there is a personal God, who rules the universe and who communicates his will to man only through "chosen" prophets. These three religions insist that they are the only monotheists. Careful examination of their doctrines proves the exact opposite — they acknowledge the existence and powers of two opposing forces in the universe. They believe that their "good god" is not in control of their "bad god". He could, but he doesn't!?!!? If they believe that there are two independent/separate forces (Good and Bad) in the universe, then they believe in two gods, i.e. polytheism.

Egyptian Mystery Plays (Encyclopedia in Action)

Egyptian cosmology is based on coherent scientific and philosophical principles. The cosmological knowledge of Ancient Egypt was expressed in a story form, which is a superior means for expressing both physical and metaphysical concepts. Any good writer or lecturer knows that stories are better than exposition for explaining the behavior of things, because the relationships of parts to each other, and to the whole, are better maintained by the mind. Information alone is useless, unless it is transformed into understanding.

The Egyptian sagas transformed common factual nouns and adjectives (indicators of qualities) into proper but conceptual nouns. These were, in addition, personified so that they could be woven into narratives. Storytellers were especially qualified people who bore an awesome responsibility of always being — **Maa Kheru** (True of Voice).

Here are three different subjects that are explained in story forms, using four personified concepts: **Ausar** (Osiris), **Auset** (Isis), **Heru** (Horus), and **Set** (Seth):

1 - The four elements of the world (water, fire, earth, and air), as quoted from Plutarch's *Moralia, Vol. V*:

> *The Egyptians simply give the name of Ausar [Osiris] to the whole source and faculty creative of moisture, believing this to be the cause of generation and the substance of life-producing seed; and the name of Set [Typhon in Greek] they give to all that is dry, fiery, and arid, in general, and antagonistic to moisture.*
> *As the Egyptians regard the Nile as the effusion of Ausar, so they hold and believe the earth to be the body of Auset [Isis], not all of it, but so much of it as the Nile covers, fertilizing it and uniting with it. From this union they make Heru [Horus] to be born. The all-*

conserving and fostering Hora, that is the seasonable tempering of the surrounding air, is Heru [Horus].
The insidious scheming and usurpation of Set [Typhon], then, is the power of drought, which gains control and dissipates the moisture which is the source of the Nile and of its rising.

Ausar   Auset   Heru   Set

2 - The model societal framework is expressed in the legendary tale of **Ausar** and **Auset**, their son **Heru**, and his uncle, **Set** [see story text in chapter 2].

3 - The trinity/triad/triangle cosmic role is expressed in the relationship between the father (**Ausar**), mother (**Auset**), and son (**Heru**), to be analogous to the right-angle triangle 3:4:5. [See story text in chapter 3.]

The Egyptian well-crafted mystery plays are an intentionally chosen means for communicating knowledge. Meaning and the mystical experience are not tied to a literal interpretation of events. Once the inner meanings of the narratives have been revealed, they become marvels of simultaneous scientific and philosophical completeness and conciseness. The more they are studied, the richer they become. And, rooted in the narrative as it is, the part can never be mistaken for the whole, nor can its functional significance be forgotten or distorted.

Chapter 2

The Egyptian Model

All Ancient Egyptian cosmic stories are embedded with the society's social framework. In other words, the society must conduct its practices in accordance with the same cosmic principles embedded in these stories.

The most common story to all Egyptians was that of **Ausar** (Osiris) and his family. There is not a single complete Egyptian record of it, in all the recovered archeological findings. Our knowledge of this legend comes from several versions that were written by the early Greek and Roman writers. The most common was the one told by Plutarch.

A shortened version of the story of the Egyptian role model goes as follows:

The self-created **Atum** spat out the twins **Shu** and **Tefnut**, who in turn gave birth to **Nut** (the sky) and **Geb** (the earth/matter).

The union of **Nut** and **Geb** produced four children, **Ausar** (Osiris), **Auset** (Isis), **Set** (Seth), and **Nebt-Het** (Nepthys).

The story goes that **Ausar** married **Auset**, and **Set** married **Nebt-het**. **Ausar** became King of the land (Egypt) after marrying **Auset**.

- The story sets the basis for the matrilineal/matriarchal society. **Auset** is the legal heiress. [Details of matriarchal society in chapter 22.]

- The story of **Ausar** (Osiris) and **Auset** (Isis) is *the* Love Story. With **Ausar** and **Auset**, there is a harmonious polarity: brother and sister, twin souls, husband and wife. This is a reflection of the ancient and Baladi beliefs of the Two Lands [see chapter 5].

- The Ancient Egyptian word for brother and husband is the same word, **sn**, as well as the word for sister and wife, **sn.t**. Therefore, we must be cautious when encountering **sn** and **sn.t** in certain texts, and not to draw too many conclusions about incest and the like.

Both **Ausar** (Osiris) and **Auset** were adored by the Egyptians. But their brother **Set** (Seth) hated **Ausar** and was jealous of his popularity. **Set** managed to pick a fight with **Ausar**, murdered him, and cut his body into 14 pieces (one for each night of the waning moon), which he scattered all over Egypt.

Ausar is associated with the waxing and waning of the moon and the cyclical nature of the universe. [More about this is shown throughout this book.]

Auset went searching for the scattered parts of her beloved **Ausar**.

One re-members and re-collects in order to heal, and in order never to forget. **Auset** wanted to put **Ausar** together, so as to put herself together, i.e. to bring about union within herself.

After **Ausar's** death, **Set**, as the husband of **Nebt-het**, became the King of Egypt, and ruled as a tyrant.

Ausar's faithful wife **Auset** found every part of her husband's body, except the phallus, which had been swallowed by a fish. She assembled his body, making the first Egyptian mummy.

At the time of his death, **Ausar** and **Auset** had no children, but by mystical means, the re-membered mummy of **Ausar** was resurrected for one night and slept with **Auset** (This is equivalent to being impregnated by the Holy Ghost). As a result, **Auset** conceived a son. He was called **Heru** (Horus) and was raised secretly in the marshes of the Nile Delta.

- This action symbolizes reincarnation and spiritual rebirth — a key to understanding the Egyptian belief in life after death.
- The *supernatural conception* and the *virgin birth* of **Heru** found their way into christianity.

When **Set** heard about the new child (**Heru**), **Set** went to kill the newborn. Hearing that **Set** was coming, **Auset** hid her son in Buto.

This is the source of the story in which Herod, upon hearing about the birth of the biblical Jesus, set out to destroy all the newborn males.

As soon as **Heru** (Horus) had grown to manhood, he challenged **Set** for the right to the throne. **Heru** and **Set** had several battles and challenges. Finally, both **Heru** (the resurrected **Ausar**) and his uncle **Set** went to the council of **neteru** to determine who should rule. Both presented their cases.

The council of **neteru** decided that **Ausar/Heru** should regain the throne of Egypt, and **Set** should rule over the deserts/wastelands.

- Physical force did not decide the outcome of the "Great Quarrel" (the struggle between **Heru** and **Set**), rather a jury of their peers (council of **neteru**) settled the matter.

I • Compromise and the principle of co-existence ended the conflict.

During the battle, **Set** snatched away the eye of **Heru**, and threw it into the celestial ocean. **Tehuti** (Thoth) recovered the eye which was later identified with the moon and became a very popular symbol of protection. It was this Eye that **Heru** used to revive his sleeping father. **Ausar** was resurrected as a soul to rule the Netherworld. **Ausar** became for the Egyptians the spirit of the past, the **neter** (god) of the Dead and a hope for resurrection and afterlife.

Another version of the story indicates that as soon as she heard of this tragedy, **Auset**(Isis) set out to search for the fragments of her husband's body, embalmed them with the help of the **neter, Anbu**(Anubis), and buried them wherever they were found and built shrines at these locations. According to this version of the story, the head of **Ausar**(Osiris)was buried at **Abtu**(Abydos). The heart was buried on the island of Philae, near Aswan. The phallus was thrown into the Nile and was swallowed by a fish. For this reason the eating of fish was forbidden to the priests.

The similarities between the Egyptian **Ausar/Auset/Heru** (Osiris/Isis/Horus) *mystery play* and the Gospel story are striking. Both accounts are practically the same, e.g. the supernatural conception, the divine birth, the struggles against the enemy in the wilderness, and the resurrection from the dead to eternal life.

The main difference between the two accounts is that those faithful to the bible consider the Gospel tale to be a historical fact, while the Ancient Egyptians considered the **Ausar/Auset/Heru** story to be — a story (parable).

Chapter 3

All Is Number

The Ancient Egyptians had a scientific and organic system of observing reality. Modern-day science is based on observing everything as dead (inanimate). Modern physical formulas in our science studies almost always exclude the vital phenomena throughout statistical analyses. For the Ancient and Baladi Egyptians, the universe — in whole and in part — is animated.

In the animated world of Ancient Egypt, numbers did not simply designate quantities but instead were considered to be concrete definitions of energetic formative principles of nature. The Egyptians called these energetic principles **neteru** (gods).

For Egyptians, numbers were not just odd and even — they were male and female. Every part of the universe was/ is a male or a female. There is no neutral (a thing). Unlike in English, where something is he, she, or it, in Egypt there was only he or she.

Egyptians manifested their knowledge of number mysticism in all aspects of their lives. The evidence that Egypt possessed this knowledge is commanding. As examples:

1 - The concept of animated numbers in Ancient Egypt were eloquently referred to by Plutarch, in *Moralia Vol. V*, describing the 3:4:5 triangle:

The upright, therefore, may be likened to the male, the base to the female, and the hypotenuse to the child of both, and so Ausar [Osiris] may be regarded as the origin, Auset [Isis] as the recipient, and Heru [Horus] as perfected result. Three is the first perfect odd number: four is a square whose side is the even number two; but five is in some ways like to its father, and in some ways like to its mother, being made up of three and two. And panta [all] is a derivative of pente [five], and they speak of counting as "numbering by fives". Five makes a square of itself.

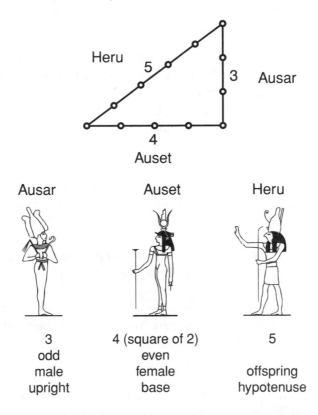

Ausar	Auset	Heru
3	4 (square of 2)	5
odd	even	
male	female	offspring
upright	base	hypotenuse

The vitality and the interactions between these numbers show how they are male and female, positive and negative, vertical and horizontal, ...etc.

2 -   Plutarch noted that One is not an (odd) number when he wrote, *three is the first perfect odd number.* For the Egyptians, one was not a number, but the essence of the underlying principle of number, all other numbers being made of it. One represents Unity: the Absolute as unpolarized energy. One is neither odd nor even but both, because if added to an odd number it makes it even, and vice-versa. So it combines the opposites of odd and even, and all the other opposites in the universe. Unity is a perfect, eternal, undifferentiated consciousness.

3 -   The Ancient Egyptian method of writing the numbers reflects their total understanding of the cosmic functions of each number. Their numbers were not abstracts like our "modern" numbers. [A few examples will explain this point, in the next chapters.]

4 -   The heading of the Ancient Egyptian papyrus known as the *Rhind (so-called "Mathematical") Papyrus* (1848-1801 BCE) reads,

> *"Rules for enquiring into nature and for knowing all that exists, every mystery, every secret".*

The intent is very clear — that Ancient Egyptians believed and set the rules for numbers and their interactions (so-called mathematics) as the basis for "all that exists".

Egyptological academia misses the forest AND the trees — splitting hair over what they perceive as merely mathematical exercises in these papyri. What is even worse, is that these academicians have no knowledge of the practical application of "mathematics" in real life.

5 - The Ancient Egyptian mode of calculation had a direct relationship with natural processes, as well as metaphysical ones. Even the language employed in the Egyptian papyri serves to promote this sense of vitality, of living interaction. We see this understanding as an example in Item no. 38 of the Egyptian papyrus known as the *Rhind (so-called "Mathematical") Papyrus*, which reads,

> *"I go three times into the hekat (a bushel, unit of volume), a seventh of me is added to me and I return fully satisfied."*

6 - The famous Ancient Egyptian hymn of *Leiden Papyrus J350* confirms that number symbolism had been practiced in Egypt, at least since the Old Kingdom (2575-2150 BCE). The *Leiden Papyrus* consists of an extended composition, describing the principle aspects of the ancient creation narratives. The system of enumeration, in the Papyrus, identifies the principle/aspect of creation and matches each one with its symbolic number.

This Egyptian Papyrus consists of 27 stanzas, numbered from 1 to 9, then from 10 to 90 in tens, then from 100 to 900 in hundreds; only 21 have been preserved. The first word of each is a sort of pun on the number concerned.

The numbering system of this Egyptian Papyrus by itself is significant. The numbers 1 to 9, and then the powers 10, 20, 30, etc., now come to constitute the energetic foundations of physical forms.

The different parts of the *Leiden Papyrus* will be discussed in conjunction with number mysticism/evaluation in the next chapters.

7 - The Ancient Egyptian name for the largest temple in Egypt, namely the Karnak Temple complex, is **Apet-sut**, which means **Enumerator of the Places**. The temple's name speaks for itself. This temple started in the Middle Kingdom in ca. 1971 BCE, and was added to continuously for the next 1,500 years. The design and enumeration, in this temple, are consistent with the creation numerical codes.

The Egyptian concept of number symbolism was subsequently popularized in the West by and through the Greek Pythagoras (ca. 580-500 BCE). It is a known fact that Pythagoras studied for about 20 years in Egypt, soon after Egypt was open to Greek *exploration* and *immigration* (in the 7th century BCE).

Pythagoras and his immediate followers left nothing of their own writing. Yet, Western Academia attributed to Pythagoras and the so-called *Pythagoreans*, an open-ended list of major achievements. They were issued a blank check by Western academia.

Pythagoras and his followers are said to see numbers as divine concepts, ideas of the God who created a universe of infinite variety, and satisfying order, to a numerical pattern.

The same principles were stated more than 13 centuries before Pythagorus' birth, in the heading of the Egyptian's *Rhind Papyrus*, which promises,

"Rules for enquiring into nature and for knowing all that exists, every mystery, every secret".

•   •   •

Some of the numbers and their symbolic significance will be described briefly in the following chapters.

Part

The Creation Numerical Codes

Chapter 4

In The Beginning

Nun, The Subjective Being

Every Egyptian creation text begins with the same basic belief that before the beginning of things, there was a liquidy *primeval abyss* — everywhere, endless, and without boundaries or directions. Egyptians called this cosmic ocean/watery chaos, **Nu/Ny/Nun** — the unpolarized state of matter.

Scientists agree with the Ancient Egyptian description of the origin of the universe as being an abyss. Scientists refer to this abyss as *neutron soup,* where there are neither electrons nor protons, and only neutrons forming one huge extremely dense nucleus. Such *chaos,* in the pre-creation state, was caused by the compression of matter, i.e. atoms did not exist in their normal states, but were squeezed so closely together, that many atomic nuclei were crowded into a space previously occupied by a single *normal* atom. Under such conditions, the electrons of these atoms were squeezed out of their orbits and move about freely (a degenerate state).

Nu/Ny/Nun is the "Subjective Being", the symbol of the *unformed, undefined, undifferentiated* energy/matter, inert or inactive, the uncreated state before the creation; it cannot be the cause of its transformation.

Ma-at, The Cosmic Order

For the deeply religious people of Egypt, the creation of the universe was not a physical event (Big Bang) that just happened. It was an orderly event that was pre-planned and executed according to an orderly Divine Law that governs the physical and metaphysical worlds. So, we read in the **Book of Knowing the Creations of Ra and Overcoming Apep** (Apophis), known as the *Bremner-Rhind Papyrus*:

> *"I had not yet found a place upon which I could stand. I conceived the Divine Plan of Law or Order (Maa) to make all forms. I was alone, I had not yet emitted Shu, nor had I yet emitted Tefnut, nor existed any other who could act together with me."*

Ma-at is the **netert** (goddess) that personifies the principle of cosmic order. The concept by which not only men, but also the **neteru** (gods) themselves were governed and without which the **neteru** (gods) are functionless.

Amen, The Occult Force

Egyptians reasoned that one could explain creation not from within creation, but only from outside it. The Creator is not the created universe. In the Egyptian papyrus known as the *Leiden Papyrus*, the **neter** (god), **Amen/Amon/Amun** (which means *hidden*), represents the hidden or occult force underlying creation. He is the *Breath of Life*. Even though he is indefinable himself, he is the reason why the universe can be defined.

The closest Egyptian term to *God* is **Amen-Renef** (*He Whose Real Essence is Unknown*).

The Becoming One

Creation is the sorting out (giving definition to / bringing order to) all the chaos (the undifferentiated energy/matter and consciousness) of the primeval state. All of the Ancient Egyptian accounts of creation exhibited this with well-defined, clearly demarcated stages.

The first stage was the self-creation of the Supreme Being as creator and Being, i.e. the passage from Subjective Being (**Nu/Ny/Nun**) to Objective Being (**Atum**). In simple human terms, this is equivalent to the moment that one passes from sleeping (unconscious state, subjective being) to being aware of oneself (gaining consciousness, objective being). It is like standing on solid ground.

Ra-Atum

This stage of creation was represented by the Egyptian sages as **Atum** rising out of **Nu/Ny/Nun**. In the Unas (so-called *Pyramid*) Texts, there is the following invocation:

Salutation to thee, Atum,
Salutation to thee, he who comes into being by himself!
Thou art high in this thy name High Mound,
Thou comest into being in this thy name Khepri (Becoming One). [§1587]

•   •   •

The sequence of creation is found in many Ancient Egyptian texts. The most detailed and clearly described sequence is found in the above-mentioned *Bremner-Rhind Papyrus*, dating from the 4th century BCE (and believed to be a reproduction from an Old Kingdom text, based on its writing style). A portion of this papyrus, known as the **Book of Knowing the Creations of Ra and Overcoming Apep** (Apophis), reads in part:

- *I conceived in my own heart; there came into being a vast number of forms of divine beings as the forms of children and the forms of their children. . . .*
- *I it was who aroused desire with my hand; I masturbated with my hand, I poured out of my mouth. I spat out Shu, I spat out Tefnut.. . . .*
- *After having become one neter (god), there were (now) three neteru (gods) in me.. . . .*
- *I created all snakes, and all that came into being with them."*

The text above refers to the Ancient Egyptians concepts (among other things) of:

1 - Creation as a Big Bang, with the separation of parts (children) and smaller Parts (their children):
> *there came into being a vast number of forms of divine beings as the forms of children and the forms of their children. . .*

2 - The duality of creation symbolized by Shu and Tefnut:
> *I spat out Shu, I spat out Tefnut.*

3 - The concept of trinity:
> *After having become one neter (god), there were [now] three neteru (gods) in me.*

4 - Creation of space/volume, wherein the universe must be manifested:
> *I created all snakes, and all that came into being with them.*

Snakes are the symbol of delineation of space.

Chapter 5

The Dualistic Nature

The world, as we know it, is held together by a law that is based on the balanced dual nature of all things (wholes, units). Among noticable balanced pairs are: male and female, odd and even, negative and positive, active and passive, light and darkness, yes and no, true and false — each pair represents a different aspect of the same fundamental principle of polarity. And each aspect partakes of the nature of unity and of the nature of duality. Sample Egyptian applications of the universal dual nature include:

1 - The pre-creation state consisted of four pairs of primeval dual-gendered twins. [See chapter 11.]

2 - The Egyptians perceived the universe in terms of a dualism between **Ma-at** — Truth and Order — and disorder. **Amen-Renef** summoned the cosmos out of undifferentiated chaos, by distinguishing the two, by giving voice to the ultimate ideal of Truth. **Ma-at**, as shown here, is usually portrayed in the double form — **Maati**.

3 -   The dual principle in the creation state was expressed in the pair of **Shu** and **Tefnut**. The pair of husband and wife is the characteristic Egyptian way of expressing duality and polarity. This dual nature was manifested in Ancient Egyptian texts and traditions, since its recovered archeological findings. The most ancient texts of the Old Kingdom, namely the *Pyramid Texts* §*1652*, express the dual nature:

Tefnut   Shu

> *...and though didst spit out as Shu, and didst spit out as Tefnut.*

This is a very powerful analogy, because we use the term "spitting image" to mean exactly like the origin.

Another way of expressing the intent of the dual nature is present in the Ancient Egyptian text, known as the *Bremner-Rhind Papyrus*:

> *I was anterior to the Two Anteriors that I made, for I had priority over the Two Anteriors that I made, for my name was anterior to theirs, for I made them anterior to the Two Anteriors ...*

4 -   **Neheb Kau** — meaning *the provider of forms/attributes* — was the name given to the serpent representing the primordial serpent in Ancient Egypt. **Neheb Kau** is depicted as a two-headed serpent, indicative of the dual spiral nature of the universe.

5 - The Egyptian Pharaoh was always referred to as the *Lord of the Two Lands*. Western academia cavalierly stated that the *Two Lands* are *Upper* and *Lower Egypt*. There is not a single Ancient Egyptian reference to confirm their notion, or even to define such a frontier between *Upper* and *Lower* Egypt.

Throughout Ancient Egyptian temples, you will find numerous symbolic representations relating to the ceremony of *Uniting the Two Lands*, where two **neteru** are shown tying the papyrus and lotus plants. Neither plant is native to any specific area in Egypt. The most common  representation shows the twin **neteru**, **Hapi** (a mirror-image of each other), each as unisex with one breast.

The term, *Two Lands*, is very familiar to the Baladi Egyptians, who refer to it in their daily life. It is their strong belief that there are *Two Lands* — the one we live on, and another one where our identical twins (of the opposite sex) live. The two are subject to the same experiences from date of birth to date of death. [More about this concept throughout this book, and particularly chapter 21.]

You and your "Siamese" twin, who "apparently" separate at birth, will re-unite again at the moment of death. The Baladi Egyptian Enumerators describe, in their lamentations after the death of a person, how the deceased is being prepared to join his/her counterpart (of the opposite sex), AS IF it is a marriage ceremony. This is reminiscent of the many symbolic illustrations in Ancient Egypt of the tying the knot of the *Two Lands*. To be married is to tie the knot.

As far back as the Unas (so-called *"Pyramid"*) Texts, one finds that the Pharaoh Unas (2356-2323 BCE) unites/joins with **Auset** (Isis) immediately after departing the earthly realm. This is based on the premise that since every man is **Ausar** in his "dead" form, each joins his/her counterpart (**Auset** in the case of a man), at the moment of the earthly departure.

6 -   The perpetual cycle of existence — the cycle of life and death — is symbolized by **Ra** (Re) and **Ausar** (Osiris). **Ra** is the living **neter** who descends into death to become **Ausar** — the **neter** of the dead. **Ausar** ascends and comes to life again as **Ra**. The creation is continuous: it is a flow of life progressing towards death. But out of death, a new **Ra** is to be born, sprouting new life. **Ra** is the cosmic principle of energy that moves toward death, and **Ausar** represents the process of rebirth. Thus, the terms of life and death become interchangeable: life means slow dying, death means resurrection to new life. The dead person in death is identified with **Ausar**, but he will come to life again, and be identified with **Ra**.

The perpetual cycle of **Ausar** and **Ra** dominates the Ancient Egyptian texts, such as:

- In *The Book of the Coming Forth By Light*, both **Ausar** and **Ra** live, die, and are born again. In the Netherworld, the souls of **Ausar** and **Ra** meet [see illustration from the **Papyrus of Ani**, on the next page], and are united to form an entity, described so eloquently:
   I am His Two Souls in his Twins.

   In Chapter 17 of *The Book of the Coming Forth By Light*, the deceased, identified with **Ausar**, says:
   I am yesterday, I know the morrow.

Ra   Ausar

And the Egyptian commentary to this passage explains:
What is this?—Ausar is yesterday, Ra is tomorrow?

- In the tomb of Queen Nefertari (wife of Ramses II), is a well known representation of the dead solar **neter** (god), as a mummiform body with the head of a ram, accompanied by an inscription, right and left:
  This is Ra who comes to rest in Ausar.
  This is Ausar who comes to rest in Ra.

- The *Litany of Ra* is basically a detailed amplification of a short passage of Chapter 17 of *The Book of the Coming Forth by Light*, describing the merging of **Ausar** and **Ra** into a Twin Soul.

7 - The eternal opposites, **Set** (Seth) and **Heru** (Horus), are assigned equal roles in representations of symbolic rites, relating to the ceremony of *Uniting the Two Lands*, which is portrayed on the limestone reliefs in Lisht, near **Men-Nefer** (Memphis). The symbolism is powerful, for the two opposites are the One in a polarized state, whereby **Set**

Heru   Set

personifies the *unevolved* desire, and **Heru** represents the *evolving* desire.

8 - Both **Heru** and **Tehuti** are shown in numerous illustrations in the Ancient Egyptian temples, performing the symbolic *Uniting of the Two Lands*. **Heru** personifies conscience, mind, intellect, and is identified with the heart. **Tehuti** personifies manifestation and deliverance, and is identified with the tongue.

Heru   Tehuti

One thinks with the heart, and acts with the tongue. These two complimentary requirements were described on the Shabaka Stele (716-701 BCE):

> *The Heart thinks all that it wishes, and the Tongue delivers all that it wishes.*

9 - One of the Egyptian King's title was *Lord of the Diadem of the Vulture and of the Serpent.* The diadem is the earthly symbol of the divine man, the King. The diadem consists of the serpent (symbol of the divine intellec-  tual function), and the vulture (symbol of the recon- ciliation function). The serpent represents intellect, the faculty by which man can break down the whole into its constituent parts, just like a serpent that swallows its prey in whole, and then digests it by breaking it down into digestible parts.

The divine man must be able both to distinguish and to reconcile. Since these dual powers reside in man's brain, the form of the serpent's body (in the diadem) follows the actual physiological sutures of the brain, in which these particularly human faculties are seated. This dual function of the brain is vivid in its two sides.

The part of the diadem located in the middle of the forehead represents the third eye, with all its intellec- tual faculties.

Chapter 6

The Triangulation of Creation

The physical and metaphysical role of Three was recognized in Ancient Egypt; for each unity is a *triple power* and a *double nature*. This was eloquently illustrated in the Ancient Egyptian texts and traditions, whereby the self-created **neter** (god), **Atum**, spat out **Shu** and **Tefnut**, then placed his arms around them, and his **ka** entered into them, to become One again. It is the Three that are Two that are One. This action generated the First Trinity, the first building block. This is made clear in the Ancient Egyptian papyrus known as the *Bremner-Rhind Papyrus,*

> *After having become one neter (god), there were [now] three neteru (gods) in me [i.e. **Atum**, **Shu**, and **Tefnut**].*

In the Ancient Egyptian texts, **Shu** and **Tefnut** are described as the ancestors of all the **neteru** (gods/goddesses) who begat all beings in the universe. This triangulation of **Atum-Shu-Tefnut** ensured a continuous relationship between the Creator and all subsequent created.

The concept of trinity in Ancient Egypt is also found in the following examples:

1 - Stanza 300 of the Ancient Egyptians' *Leiden Papyrus* declares the unity in one Being of the three principles, **Amen**, **Ra**, and **Ptah**. Stanza 300 reads in part:

> *"Three are all the neteru: Amen, Ra, Ptah...his hidden name is Amen. Ra belongs to him as his face, Ptah is his body".*

A stunning example of a Holy Trinity.

2 - Other examples of familiar Ancient Egyptian triads are:

> *Amen - Mut - Khonsu*
> *Ausar (Osiris) - Auset (Isis) - Heru (Horus)*
> *Ptah - Sekhmet - Nefertum*
> *Ptah - Sokar - Ausar (Osiris)*

3 - The triple shrine is the main feature in most Egyptian temples, to enshrine the triple power (three **neteru**) of each temple.

4 - Each small locality in Ancient Egypt had its own triad of **neteru**, i.e. identifiable building block. These local triads were not in conflict with each other — they were the metaphysical building blocks of each locality.

5 - For the Ancient Egyptians, Three/Triads/Trinities/Triangles are one and the same. There was no functional difference between geometric triangles, musical triads, or any of the many trinities of Ancient Egypt. The clearest example was explained by Plutarch regarding the 3:4:5 triangle, in *Moralia Vol V*:

> *The Egyptians hold in high honor the most beautiful of the triangles, since they liken the nature of the Universe most closely to it...* [see more of text on pgs 28,29.]

In other words, triangles in their different forms represent different natures in the universe.

Chapter 7

The Stability of Four

IIII

Four is the number signifying solidity and stability. The significance of the number 4 is shown in the following examples from Ancient Egypt:

1 - Egyptian texts state that the pre-creation chaos possessed characteristics that were identified with four pairs of primordial powers/forces. Each pair represents the primeval dual-gendered twins — the masculine/feminine aspect. The four pairs are equivalent to the four forces of the universe (the weak force, the strong force, gravity, and electromagnetism).

2 - Ancient Egyptians had four main cosmological teaching centers at: **Onnu** (*Heliopolis*), **Men-Nefer** (*Memphis*), **Ta-Apet** (*Thebes*), and **Khmunu** (*Hermopolis*). Each center revealed one of the principle phases or aspects of genesis.

   The four pairs of the pre-creation state are a constant theme at all four centers.

   Egypt now has 4 Sufi Teaching Ways, which were created in the 11th century CE, to maintain the Ancient Egyptian traditions under the islamic rule.

3 - Egyptians used the four simple phenomena (fire, air,
     earth and water) to describe the functional roles of the
     four elements necessary to matter. Water is the sum —
     the composite principle of fire, earth and air. Water is
     also a substance over and above them.

     These concepts were expressed in the Ancient Egyp-
     tian texts as **Nu/Nun**, the primeval (liquid) water that
     contains all elements of the universe. Plutarch con-
     firmed that about Ancient Egyptians, in his *Moralia*,
     Vol V:

> *For the nature of water, being the source and origin of
> all things, created out of itself three primal material
> substances: Earth, Air, and Fire.*

     [Read the text regarding the four elements in Ancient Egypt
     in Chapter 1.]

4 - Stanza 40 of the Ancient Egyptians' *Leiden Papyrus* in-
     troduces the 'Becoming', telling of the Divine Crafts-
     man of the universe, symbolized as **Ptah**, *The Manifester
     of Forms*. [For more on **Ptah**, see chapter 16.]

5 - The **Tet** (Djed) pillar, symbol of the sup-
     port of creation, has four elements.

6 - Other applications are: the four children
     of the **neter** (god) *Geb* (the earth), the 4
     cardinal points, the 4 regions of the sky,
     the 4 pillars of the sky (material support
     of the realm of the spirit), the 4 sons of
     Heru (Horus), the 4 canopic jars into
     which the 4 organs were placed after
     death.

The **Tet** Pillar

Chapter 8

The Fifth Star

The significance and function of number five, in Ancient Egypt, is indicated by the manner in which it was written. The number 5 in Ancient Egypt was written as 2 (II) above 3 (III), or as a five-pointed star. In other words, number 5 is the result of the relationship between number 2 and number 3.

Two symbolizes the power of multiplicity, the female, mutable receptacle, while Three symbolizes the male. This was the 'music of the spheres', the universal harmonies played out between these two primal male and female universal symbols of **Ausar** (Osiris) and **Auset** (Isis), whose heavenly marriage produced the child, **Heru** (Horus). Plutarch confirmed this Egyptian wisdom in *Moralia Vol V*:

> *Three [Osiris] is the first perfect odd number: four is a square whose side is the even number two [Isis]; but five [Horus] is in some ways like to its father, and in some ways like to its mother, being made up of three and two. And panta (all) is a derivative of pente (five), and they speak of counting as "numbering by fives".*

Five incorporates the principles of polarity (II) and reconciliation (III). All phenomena, without exception, are polar in nature, treble in principle. Therefore, five is the key

to the understanding of the manifested universe, as per
Plutarch, on the Egyptian thinking.

And panta *(all) is a derivative of* pente *(five).*

Stanzas 50 and 500 of the Ancient Egyptians' *Leiden
Papyrus*, whose first word **dua** means at the same time *five*
and *to worship*, consist of hymns of adoration exalting the
marvels of Creation.

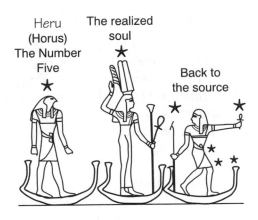

In Ancient Egypt, the symbol for a star was drawn with
five points. The Star was the Egyptian symbol for both des-
tiny and the number five.

The five-pointed stars are the homes of the successfully
departed souls, as stated in the *Unas Funerary Texts* (known
as *Pyramid Texts*), Line 904:

be a soul as a living star ...

Heru (Horus) is the personification of the goal of all
initiated teachings, and therefore is associated with the number five, for he is the fifth, after **Ausar, Auset, Set** and **Nebt-
het. Heru** is also the number 5 in the right angle triangle of
3:4:5, as confirmed by Plutarch.

Chapter 9

The Cubical Sixth

Stanza 6 of the Ancient Egyptian *Leiden Papyrus* is the first that remains intact of the unit series of numbers 1-9. Because of the six directions, 6 is the number *par excellence* of space, volume and time, and thus this stanza deals with all the regions which are under the dominion of Amen-Ra.

Six is the cosmic number of the material world and therefore is the number chosen by the Egyptians to symbolize both time and space. Time and space are two sides of the same coin, which is perfectly represented in the science of astronomy and its application — astrology. Scientists now agree that there is a very close connection between space and time — so close that you can't have one without the other.

1 - **Time** - Anything to do with timekeeping, for the Ancient Egyptians, was and is based on the number six, or its multiples. The whole day was/is 24 (6 x 4) hours, consisting of 12 (6 x 2) hours of daytime, and 12 (6 x 2) hours of nighttime. The hour was/is 60 (6 x 10) minutes, and the minute was/is 60 seconds. The month was/is 30 days (6 x 5). The year was/is 12 months (6 x 2). The Great Zodiac Year contained 12 Zodiac Ages (signs).

2 - **Space (Volume)** - requires 6 directions of extension to define it: up and down, backwards and forwards, left and right. The cube, the perfect 6-sided figure, was used in Egypt as the symbol for space (volume).

The Egyptian was highly conscious of the box-like structure, which is the model of the earth or the material world. The form of statuary called the *"cube statue"* are prevalent since the Middle Kingdom (2040-1783 BCE). The subject was integrated into the cubic form of the stone. In these cube statues, there is a powerful sense of the subject emerging from the prison of the cube.  Its symbolic significance is that the spiritual principle is emerging from the material world. The earthly person is placed unmistakably in material existence.

The Divine person is shown sitting squarely on a cube i.e. mind over matter.

Other traditions, such as the *Platonic* and *Pythagorean*, adopted the same concept of the Egyptian cubic representation of the material world.

So, the symbolism of "thinking outside the box", and to "try to get out of the box" (in the theatrical mime performance), are originally Egyptian practices.

Chapter 10

The Cyclical Seven

The significance and function of the number 7 in Ancient Egypt is indicated by how they wrote it. Since 7 signified the union of spirit (Three III) and matter (Four IIII), it was accordingly written in such format (shown here). One of the forms that traditionally expresses the meaning of 7 is the pyramid, which combines the square base symbolizing the four elements, and the triangular sides symbolizing the three modes of spirit.

Ausar is the 7th in the process of creation: **Nun, Atum, Shu, Tefnut, Geb, Nut** and **Ausar**. It is **Ausar** who is the first born of the union of heaven (**Nut**) and earth (**Geb**), i.e. the union of spirit (**Nut**) and matter (**Geb**).

It is therefore that **Ausar** (Osiris) is associated with the number 7 and its multiples. Seven is the number of process, growth, and the underlying cyclical aspects of the universe.

Seven of something frequently makes a complete set — the 7 days of the week, 7 colors of the spectrum, 7 notes of the musical scale, etc. The cells of the human body are totally renewed every 7 years.

The intimate relationship between **Ausar** and 7 is reflected in these few examples, from the Temple of **Ausar** at **Abtu** (Abydos):

1 - It is the only temple that has 7 chapels.

2 - There are 7 spirit forms of **Ausar**.

3 - There are 7 boats of **Ausar**.

4 - 42 (7x6) is the number of assessors/jurors on Judgment Day, where **Ausar** presides.

5 - 42 (7x6) is the number of steps leading to this temple.

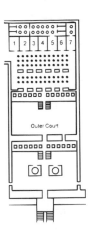

•   •   •

The **Tet** (Djed) pillar, as the sacred symbol of **Ausar**, has 7 steps. This is reminiscent of the doctrine of chakras in the Indian kundalini system of yoga, that is much younger than the Ancient Egyptian traditions. The chakras are centers in the psychophysical structure of man that accord with the 7 constituents of man, along with the link that draws them together, namely the human backbone.

The 7 centers of **Tet** (Djed) represent the 7 metaphorical rungs of the ladder, leading from matter to spirit. Since man is a microcosm of the cosmic pattern, **Tet** represents a microcosm of the universal cosmology.

It is hard to separate the number 7 from **Ausar**. [More relationships will be detailed in later chapters, especially chapter 17.]

Chapter 11

Eight, The Octave

Seven is the end of a cycle. Eight is the beginning of a new cycle — an octave.

As will be detailed in the next chapter, Ancient and Baladi Egyptians believe that the universe consists of 9 realms (7 heavens and 2 lands/earths). Our earthly existence is the 8th realm (first land/earth).

At number 8, we find the human being created in the image of God, the First Principle. Our earthly existence at the 8th realm is a replication and not a duplication — an octave. Octave is the future state of the past. The continuance of creation is a series of replications — octaves.

In Egypt, the well-known text, *Coffin of Petamon* [Cairo Museum item no. 1160], states:

> *I am One who becomes Two,*
> *who becomes Four,*
> *who becomes Eight,*
> *and then I am One again.*

This new unity (**One again**) is not identical, but analogous, to the first unity (**I am One**). The old unity is no longer, a new unity has taken its place: *The King is Dead, Long Live the King.* It is a renewal or self-replication. And to account for the principle of self-replication, 8 terms are necessary.

Musically, the renewal theme of 8 terms corresponds to the *octave* because it reaches through all 8 intervals of the scale (the 8 white keys of the keyboard).

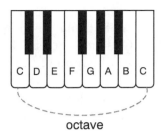

octave

For example, an octave can be 2 successive C's (*Do's*) on a musical scale, as illustrated herein on the keyboard.

Eight is the number of **Tehuti**, and at **Khmunu** (Hermopolis), **Tehuti** (*Hermes* to the Greeks, *Mercury* to the Romans) is called the *Master of the City of Eight*. **Tehuti** gives man access to the mysteries of the manifested world, which were symbolized by the number 8. As we will find out [in chapter 15], the manifestation of creation came through the word (soundwaves) delivered from **Ra** by **Tehuti**.

Stanza 80 of the Ancient Egyptian *Leiden Papyrus* retraces the Creation as told in **Khmunu** (Hermopolis), which deals with the Ogdoad — the Primordial Eight — which comprised the first metamorphosis of **Amen-Ra**, the mysterious, hidden one who is recognized as **Ta-Tenen** at **Men-Nefer** (Memphis), then **Ka-Mut-f** at **Ta-Apet** (Thebes), yet all the while remaining One.

Therefore, the manifestation of creation in 8 terms are present in all four Ancient Egyptian cosmological centers:

- At **Men-Nefer** (Memphis), **Ptah,** in his 8 forms, created the universe.

- At **Onnu**(Heliopolis), **Atum** created the 8 divine beings.

- At **Khmunu**(Hermopolis), 8 primeval *neteru* — the Ogdoad — created the universe. They were the personification of the primeval waters.

- At **Ta-Apet**(Thebes), **Amun/Aman/Amen** after creating himself in secret, created the Ogdoad.

The manifestation of creation through 8 terms is also reflected in the mystical process of squaring the circle. [More about it in chapter 15.]

Part

The Energy Matrix

Chapter 12

Animism,
The Energized Universe

Let Creation Begin

As stated earlier, the laws and nature of the created universe were pre-planned before the actual creation. About 15 billion years ago, when it was time for action, the condensed energy in **Nun** — *the neutron soup* — began building up, until it finally exploded and expanded outward. The explosion was loud enough to be called the *Big Bang*.

The Ancient Egyptian texts likewise repeatedly stressed that sound was the cause of creation. [More about sound and creation in chapter 15.]

The divine sound (*Big Bang*) transformed the potential inert energy/matter in **Nun** into the parts of the universe as differentiated, orderly, structured — kinetic energies — in the form of objects, thoughts, forces, physical phenomena, etc.

Transforming one type of energy (potential) into another type (kinetic) made the universe come to life, in whole and in its constituent parts.

It is all a matter of energies.

A Matter of Energies

The Ancient and Baladi Egyptians made/make no distinction between a metaphysical state of being and one with a material body. Such a distinction is a mental illusion. We exist on a number of different levels at once, from the most physical to the most metaphysical. Einstein agreed with the same principles.

Since Einstein's relativity theory, it has been known and accepted that matter is a form of energy — a coagulation or condensation of energy. Energy is made up of molecules rotating or vibrating at various rates of speed. In the "physical" world, molecules rotate at a very slow and constant rate of speed. That is why things appear to be solid, for our earthly senses. The slower the speed, the more dense or solid the thing. In the metaphysical (spirit) world, the molecules vibrate at a much faster, or ethereal dimension — where things are freer and less dense.

In this light, the universe is basically a hierarchy of energies, at different orders of density. Our senses have some access to the densest form of energy, which is *matter*. The hierarchy of energies is interrelated, and each level is sustained by the level below it. This hierarchy of energies is set neatly into a vast matrix of deeply interfaced natural laws. It is both physical and metaphysical.

This matrix of energies came as a result of the initial act of creation and the subsequent effects of the *Big Bang* that created the universe. This matrix of energies was identified with the **neteru** (gods/goddesses) in Ancient Egypt.

The presence of energy in everything was long recognized by the Ancient and Baladi Egyptians. That there are cosmic energies (**neteru**) in every stone, mineral, wood, etc., is stated clearly in the Shabaka Stele (8th Century BCE):

And so the neteru (gods) entered into their bodies, in the form of every sort of wood, of every sort of mineral, as every sort of clay, as everything which grows upon him (meaning earth).

The universal energy matrix (known in its pre-creation state as **Nun/Ny/Nu**), encompasses the world as a product of a complex system of relationships among people (living and dead), animals, plants, and natural and supernatural phenomena. This rationale is often called **Animism** because of its central premise that all things are *animated* (energized) by life forces. Each minute particle of everything is in constant motion, i.e. energized, as acknowledged in the kinetic theory. In other words, everything is animated (energized)— animals, trees, rocks, birds, even the air, sun, and moon.

The faster form of energies — these invisible energies in the universe — are called *spirits* by many. Spirits/energies are organized at different orders of densities, which relates to the different speeds of molecules. These faster (invisible) energies inhabit certain areas, or are associated with particular natural phenomena. Spirits (energies) exist in family-type groups (i.e. related to each other).

Energies may occupy, at will, a more condensed energy (matter), such as human, animal, plant, or any form. The spirit animates the human body at birth, and leaves it at death. Sometimes, more than one energy spirit enters a body. We often hear a person 'not feeling himself/herself', or is 'temporarily insane', 'possessed', 'beside oneself', or a person has multiple personalities. The energies (spirits) have an effect on all of us, to one degree or another.

Since the created universe is orderly, its energy matrix is likewise a well-oiled machine with nine interpenetrating and interacting realms.

The Nine Realms

Ancient and Baladi Egyptians believe that the universal energy matrix consists of nine realms, which are commonly classified as seven heavens (metaphysical realms) and two earths (physical realms). God lives in the most distant heaven. Angels (**neteru**) inhabit heavens two through six. Ancestor spirits inhabit the heaven nearest the two earths.

The two earthly realms are commonly known as *The Two Lands*. In the previous chapter, we followed the significance of the number 8, as our physical (earthly) realm. The last realm — number 9 — is where our complimentary opposite exists. The Siamese twins who live in realms 8 and 9 are in perfect harmony. In musical terms, the ratio/relationship 8:9 represents the Perfect Tone.

Beings who are more spiritually aware reside on a higher level, and less evolved souls are on a lower level. We can never go to a higher level until we earn it. However, those beings on a higher level can go to a lower sphere; and in many cases, they do just that in order to aid and assist those souls who are not as aware.

The Ancient Egyptian texts clearly allude to climbing/passing through levels/steps; an example can be found in the Unas Funerary (Pyramid) Texts at Saqqara — Utterance 215 §149, from the Sarcophagus Chamber:

> *thy arms are Hapy and Dua-mutef,*
> *which thou needest to <u>ascend to heaven</u>,*
> *and thou ascendest;*
> *thy legs are Imesty and Kebeh-senuf,*
> *which thou needest to <u>descend to the lower sky</u>,*
> *and <u>thou descendest</u>.*

The text (just one example out of many) clearly states: *"...ascend to heaven...descend to the lower sky"*.

The concept of 9 realms are consistent with the concept of the Grand Ennead — the unity of 9 — the generator of the manifested creation. [See more information about the Grand Ennead in Chapter 14.]

The energies in the 9 realms form an orderly interactive hierarchy. [Interacting between energies is shown in chapters 24, 25, 28, 29, and 30.]

The **neteru** who are in high heavens/realms will be discussed in the following chapters.

Chapter 13

Neteru, The Angels of God

Neteru and Angels

The **neteru** (gods) are the personification of the energies/powers/forces that, through their actions and interactions, created, maintained, and continue to maintain the universe.

Depiction of
Ancient Egyptian **Neteru**

The **neteru**, and their functions, were later acknowledged by others as *angels*. The Song of Moses in Deuteronomy (32:43), as found in a cave at Qumran near the Dead Sea, mentions the word **gods** in the plural: "*Rejoice, O heavens, with him; and do obeisance to him, ye gods*". When the passage is quoted in the New Testament (Hebrews, 1:6), the word **gods** is substituted with '*angels of God*'.

The spheres of **neteru** (known also as angels and archangels in christianity) are hierarchical among the levels/realms of the universe [as described in the previous chapter].

Pictorial Symbolism of the Neteru

In order to simplify and convey the scientific and philosophical meanings of the **neteru** (gods), some fixed representations were utilized. As a result, the figures of **Ptah**, **Ausar** (Osiris), **Amen**, **Heru** (Horus), **Mut**, etc., became the signs of such attributes/functions/forces/energies.

These pictorial symbols were intended merely to fix the attention or represent abstract ideas, and were not intended to be looked upon as real personages.

A symbol, by definition, is not what it represents, but what it stands for, what it suggests. A symbol reveals to the mind a reality other than itself. Words convey information; symbols evoke understanding.

A chosen symbol represents that function or principle, on all levels simultaneously — from the simplest, most obvious physical manifestation of that function to the most abstract and metaphysical. Without recognizing the simple fact about the intent of symbolism, we will continue to be ignorant of the wealth of Egyptian knowledge and wisdom.

In Egyptian symbolism, the precise role of the **neteru** (gods) was revealed in many ways: by dress, headdress, crowns, feathers, animal, plant, color, position, size, gesture, sacred object, or type of symbolic equipment (e.g., flail, scepter, staff, ankh). This symbolic language represents a

A picture like this is worth a thousand words.

wealth of physical, physiological, psychological and spiritual data in the symbols.

Animals' Power

Egyptians' careful observation and profound knowledge of the natural world enabled them to identify certain animals with specific qualities that could symbolize certain divine functions and principles, in a particularly pure and striking fashion. As such, certain animals were chosen as symbols for that particular aspect of divinity.

This effective mode of expression is consistent with all cultures, for in the West (for example) they would say *quiet as a mouse, sly like a fox* ,...etc. Therefore, animal representation of functions and attributes is very powerful indeed.

The animal or animal-headed **neteru** (gods) were symbolic expressions of a deep spiritual understanding. When a total animal is presented in Ancient Egypt, it represents a particular function/attribute in its purest form. When an animal-headed figure is presented, it conveys that particular function/attribute in the human being. The two forms of **Anbu** (Anubis), in the two illustrations shown here clearly distinguishes these two aspects.

•   •   •

The Ancient Egyptian mode of writing, commonly called *hieroglyphs*, comprises a large number of pictorial symbols. The word *hieroglyph* has its origin in the Greek language, and means *holy script* (*hieros* = holy/sacred, *glyphein* = impress).

There are numerous sacred symbols (hieroglyphs) that depict animals, whole or part thereof, such as those shown below:

[Some examples of animal symbolism in Ancient Egypt are shown throughout this book. Later chapters will present a few of the **neteru** (gods) of Egypt.]

Chapter 14

Ra, Cosmic Creative Force

The One Joined Together

In Ancient Egyptian traditions, **Ra** personifies the primeval, cosmic, creative force. **The Litany** describes **Ra** as **The One Joined Together, Who Comes Out of His Own Members**. The Ancient Egyptian definition of **Ra** is the perfect representation of the Unity that comprises the putting together of the many diverse entities, i.e. *The One Who is the All*.

The Litany of Ra describes the aspects of the creative principle: being recognized as the **neteru** (gods) whose actions and interactions in turn created the universe. As such, all the Egyptian **neteru** who took part in the creation process are aspects of **Ra**. There are 75 forms or aspects of **Ra**. As such, **Ra** is often incorporated into the names of other **neteru** (gods) such as in **Amen-Ra** of **Ta-Apet** (Thebes), **Ra-Atum** of **Onnu/ Annu** (Heliopolis), **Ra-Harakhte** (shown herein), ...etc.

Ra-Harakhte

The solar energy of the sun is only one of numerous manifestations of **Ra**. That **Ra** is not just the sun (only a singular form), was also confirmed in the following verse from the Story of **Ra** and **Auset** (Isis), in which **Ra** states,
"I have multitude of names, and multitude of forms."

The Grand Ennead, The Nine Circles

Appropriately enough, the ninth Stanza of the Ancient Egyptian *Leiden Papyrus* recalls the Grand Ennead — the first nine entities that came forth from **Nun**.

The first of the Grand Ennead was **Atum**, who came into being out of **Nun** — the cosmic ocean. **Atum** then spat out the twins **Shu** and **Tefnut**, who in turn gave birth to **Nut** and *Geb*, whose union produced **Ausar** (Osiris), **Auset** (Isis), **Set** (Seth) and **Nebt-Het**(Nephthys).

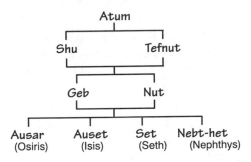

The nine aspects of the Grand Ennead emanate from, and are circumscribed about, The Absolute. They are not a sequence, but a unity — interpenetrating, interacting, and interlocked. They are the generator of all creation, as symbolized by **Heru** (Horus), who according to the *Leiden Papyrus*, Stanza No. 50, is:

...the offspring of the nine-times-unity of neteru.

Since the human being is a universal replica, a human child is normally conceived, formed, and born in nine months. Number 9 marks the end of gestation and the end of each series of numbers.

Heru (Horus) is also associated with the number 5 [as explained in chapter 8]. Five is the number of the cosmic solids (polyhedrons): tetrahedron, cube, octahedron, dodecahedron, and icosahedron. These 5 solids are formed from within 9 concentric circles, with each solid touching the sphere that circumscribes the next solid within it. These 9 circles represent the nine — unity of the Grand Ennead, the generator of all creation that is represented by these cosmic solids.

• • •

In the *Litany of Ra*, Ra is described as *The One of the Cat*, and as *The Great Cat*. The nine realms of the universe are manifested in the cat, for both the cat and the Grand Ennead (meaning nine-times-unity) have the same ancient Egyptian term b.st. This relationship has found its way to the Western culture, where one says that *the cat has nine lives (realms)*.

Ancient and Baladi Egyptians love The Cat and what it embodies. Herodotus wrote about the b.st temple of Bubastis, right outside Zagazig, in the Nile Delta.

"Although other Egyptian cities were carried to a great height, in my opinion the greatest mounds were thrown up about the city of Bubastis, in which is a temple of Bast well worthy of mention; for though other temples may be larger and more costly, none is more pleasing to look at than this."

The annual festivities of this ancient city attracted more than 700,000 people, singing, dancing, and having a great time. Herodotus described the joy of the people, celebrating Bast, the symbol of Joy. The cruelty of the foreign invaders reduced this marvelous place into a pile of rubble.

Scarab Symbolism

Ra is frequently represented as a large black scarab beetle, sitting in the solar boat and rolling the sun disc, or as a man whose human head is replaced by a scarab beetle. As such, Ra must be the original divine Scarab. The Egyptian name for the scarab beetle was **Khepri**, a multiple word meaning **he who brings into being.**

Horapollo Niliaeus explains the symbolism of the scarab in this way:

To signify the only begotten, or birth, or a father, or the world, or man, they [Egyptians] draw a scarab. The only begotten, because this animal is self-begotten, unborn of the female. For its birth takes place only in the following way. When the male wishes to have offspring, it takes some cow-dung and makes a round ball of it, very much in the shape of the world. Rolling it with its hind legs from east to west, it faces the east, so as to give it the shape of the world, for the world is borne from the east to the west.

In the elaborate symbolism of the transformational (funerary) texts, the dead King, identified with **Ausar** (Osiris), passed through analogous stages in the night of the underworld and was reborn as a new **Ra**, in his form of **Khepri** (the scarab beetle) in the morning. The analogy to the sun — disappearing at night and appearing in glory in the morning — is clear. The scarab was the symbol of the transforming quality of the sun, the light that becomes out of darkness.

Chapter 15

Tehuti, The Divine Tongue

The Sound and the Form

Egyptian creation texts repeatedly stress the belief of creation by the Word. When nothing existed except the One, he created the universe with his commanding voice. The Egyptian *Book of the Coming Forth by Light* (wrongly and commonly translated as the *Book of the Dead*), the oldest written text in the world, states:

Tehuti

> I am the Eternal ... I am that which created the Word ... I am the Word ...

In Ancient Egypt, the *words* of **Ra**, revealed through **Tehuti** (equivalent to *Hermes* or *Mercury*), became the things and creatures of this world, i.e. the words (meaning sound waves) created the forms in the universe.

The *word* (any word) is scientifically a vibrational complex element, which is a wave phenomenon, characterized by movement of variable frequency and intensity. In other words, sound is caused by compressing air particles — by rearranging the spacing and movement of air particles, i.e. creating forms. Each soundwave frequency has its own geometrical corresponding form.

Tehuti and Ra (Perfect Tone)

The word (sound) energies of **Tehuti** transformed the creation concept/impulse of **Ra** (symbolized in a circle) into a physical and metaphysical reality. Such transformation is reflected in the Ancient Egyptian process of "squaring the circle", as evident in all their numerological (so-called "mathematical") papyri. In all these papyri, the area of a circle was obtained by finding the equivalent square. The diameter was always represented as 9 cubits. The Ancient Egyptian papyri equate the 9 cubit diameter circle to a square with the sides of 8 cubits.

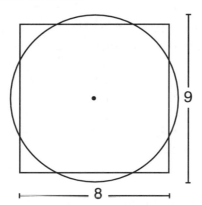

The number 9, as the diameter, represents the Grand Ennead — the group of 9 **neteru** (gods). The 9 are all aspects of **Ra**, the primeval cosmic creative force, whose symbol is/was the circle.

As stated earlier, 8 represents the manifested creation, as represented by the *Master of Eight*, namely **Tehuti**.

Musically, the ratio of 8:9 is called (appropriately enough) *The Perfect Tone*. Temple sanctuaries, such as the top sanctuary at the Luxor Temple, are an 8:9 rectangular shape.

Name Calling

As stated earlier, Egyptian creation texts repeatedly stress the belief of creation by the Word. We find that in the *Book of the Divine Cow* (found in the shrines of **Tut-Ankh-Amen**), **Ra** creates the heavens and its hosts merely by pronouncing some words whose sound alone evokes the names of things — and these things then appear at his bidding. As its name is pronounced, so the thing comes into being. For the name is a reality, the thing itself. In other words, each particular sound has/is its corresponding form, as stated earlier in this chapter.

The role of the name in Ancient and Baladi Egypt was not, as per our modern-day thinking, a mere label. The name of a **neter**, person, animal, or principle, represents a resume or synopsis of the qualities of that person or object. To know and pronounce the real name of a **neter** (god), man, or animal is to exercise power over it. It is therefore that Ancient and Baladi Egyptians have real "secret" names for everybody and everything, in order to protect the person and the thing.

The traditional story of the *Mystery of the Divine Name* is found on an Ancient Egyptian papyrus, now in the Turin Museum. In the story, **Ra** refused to tell even the most beloved Being, **Auset** (Isis), his real (secret) name. The events of the story end with **Ra** "divulging" his "secret" name as **Amen**. It should be noted that **Amen** means *secret/hidden*. In other words, under all difficult circumstances, **Ra** (as a model for all) did not divulge his real name, but only stated that his secret name was [**Amen**] secret.

The learned and most trusted people in an Egyptian community knew/know the great real (or secret) names of the **neteru** (gods) and other cosmic forces, and used this knowledge to maintain order in the world.

Most Ancient and Baladi Egyptians have at least two names — one common (official) name, and the other secret name. The person's secret name is the real name that resonates with the cosmos. The name symbolizes and embodies the individuality of the person (everything that distinguishes somebody from someone else). Naming a person in Ancient and Baladi Egypt was/is not an arbitrary choice, but was/is done in consultation with an astrologist. People also get hints of the "real" name for the new baby from ancestors: in dreams, signs, candle flickerings, etc.

The real name was/is imbued with magical powers and properties; to destroy someone's name was/is to deprive them of all individuality and all power. To perpetuate the name of the father was the son's earnest duty. According to the Egyptian traditions, one could do nothing better for anyone than to *cause his name to live* with inscriptions and representations, and nothing worse than to allow his name to perish.

Calling a person's name was/is important in performing Egyptian chants and spells. Incantation and chanting are scientifically controlled sound waves, which generate sonar fields, establishing an immediate vibratory identity with the essential principle that underlies any object or form. By pronouncing certain words or names of powers, in the proper manner and in the proper tone of voice, a priest/doctor could heal the sick, and cast out the evil spirits (in other words the contrary/incompatible energies) that caused the pain and suffering.

Ancient and Baladi Egyptians did/do not have the so-called last (sur or family) "name". Each family lineage was/is defined by its profession/trade. It was/is one's profession/trade name that determines the "family name". [More about this in chapter 23.]

Harmony of the Spheres

As per common knowledge, everything — from the smallest to the largest unit — is in constant motion. Since motion is the cause of sound (compressing air particles), it should follow that the motions of the planets must produce sound. And since the relative pitch of any musical sound is a function of the velocity of the moving object, the pitches emitted by the motions of the planets vary in accordance with their individual speeds.

With this line of reasoning, harmonics and astronomy are intimately related.

The Egyptian understanding of *universal harmony,* in an astronomical-musical sense, was confirmed by early Greek and Roman travelers. According to Diodorus:

> *Tehuti* (whom he calls by the Greek name of *Hermes*) **was the first to observe the orderly arrangement of the stars and the harmony of the musical sounds and their nature.**

In Ancient Egypt, temples were commonly provided with a complement of musicians and dancers, whose task it was to participate in the various daily and seasonal cycles of worship, so as to attune to the universal harmony.

The **neteru** (gods) themselves are depicted on the temple walls, playing musical instruments. There are also many representations of musicians, on the walls of temples, playing directly to a **neter** (god), such as to **Ptah, Heru** (Horus), **Sekhmet, Khans** and **Wazet.**

The **netert** (goddess), **Het-Heru** (Hathor), was known as the mistress of dance and the mistress of music. **Het-Heru** was the great provider of spiritual nourishment and healing. She provided joy, lovemaking, music and cheerfulness.

Het-Heru

In a hymn to **Het-Heru,** at her temple in Dendera, there is indication of the intimate relationship between music and the cosmos:

The sky and its stars make music to you.
The sun and the moon praise you.
The neteru (gods) exalt you.
The neteru (gods) sing to you.

Chapter 16

Ptah, The Divine Smith

In Ancient Egypt, **Ptah** was the cosmic shaping force, the giver of form (smith). He was the coagulating, creative fire, simultaneously the cause (of the created world) and effect (of the scission).

The role of **Ptah**, as the coagulating fire, is described in the Egyptian *Coffin Texts, Spell 1130*:

> **I am the Lord of Fire who lives on truth.**

The **truth** mentioned in the above text is **Ma-at** — the cosmic law, harmony, equilibrium. **Ptah** sits enthroned or stands upon a pedestal in the form of the glyph for **Ma-at**, to emphasize the importance of balancing energies in the transformation process, from a raw to finished form.

Ptah

The transformation process to finished form requires a delicate balance in the handling of energies. It is therefore that **Ptah** is depicted as imprisoned, bound in swaddling clothes, with only head, hands and feet free. This symbolizes **Ptah** as the coagulating fire, bound by the **neter** (god) **Set**, (principle of contraction) in the matter. Nature cannot exist without such dual opposing forces.

Ptah's main cosmological center was at **Men-Nefer** (Memphis), which was one of the four main cosmological centers in Ancient Egypt.

Ptah is/was patron of crafts, trades, and the arts. **Ptah's** counterparts on earth are the smiths, who were/are highly revered and sometimes feared, because of their supernatural powers in handling, controlling, and manipulating the four elements of creation. These four elements are always present at the smith's forge: fire, the air of the bellows to tease fire, water to tame fire, and earth, as the provider of raw materials.

The Pharaoh himself, as well as other spiritual leaders and intermediaries were/are identified with the mysterious craft of the smith.

Because of their special powers, **Ptah's** counterparts on earth (the smiths) perform the work aimed at shaping the environment and the individuals around them. The society relied on these artisans to be their intermediaries, to guide their religious upbringing, such as boys' circumcision and training [see page 147 for more information]. They also helped the rest of society to solve their problems, from the physical (e.g. fixing tools) to the metaphysical (e.g. influencing events).

The Greeks identified **Ptah** with *Hephaestus*, the divine smith. Their names may be linked etymologically. **Ptah** is also identified with the Romans' *Vulcan*.

Chapter 17

Ausar, the Resurrection

The Grand Ancestor

According to the Ancient Egyptian traditions, **Ausar** (Osiris) came to earth for the benefit of mankind, bearing the title of **Manifester of Good and Truth**.

As per the Egyptian Model Story [chapter 2], despite his mythical death and dismemberment, **Ausar** carried the living seed of eternity — **Heru** (Horus) — within him. As such, **Ausar** represents the mortal man carrying within himself the capacity and power of spiritual salvation. All dead persons were/are equated to **Ausar**, because **Ausar** is a cosmic principle, and not a historical person.

Every Egyptian's hope was/is resurrection in a transformed body and of immortality, which could only be realized through the death and resurrection of **Ausar**.

Ausar is usually represented as a mummified, bearded human body wearing the white crown. He is usually shown carrying:

1 - the shepherd's crook (being the shepherd of mankind).

2 - the flail symbolizing the ability to separate wheat from chaff.

3 - the scepter of supremacy.

One of the numerous illustrations showing the
Resurrection Principle — **Ausar**

As it was stated earlier, **Ausar** is the first born of the union of spirit (**Nut**) and matter (*Geb*) — the first human being. As such, he represents the Grand Ancestor.

The concept of **Ausar** as the Grand Ancestor extended to the Ancient and Baladi Egyptian's entire sociology and existence. From beginning to end, a long chain of ancestral precedents became a custom and a law. Every Egyptian's duty was/is to honor their ancestors with responsible actions and good deeds.

Every Egyptian learned/learns to honor his/her ancestors because s/he will be judged by them — as symbolized in **Ausar**, the Grand Ancestor, who as the great judge of the dead presides over the procedures of the Day of Judgment. [Read more about the Day of Judgment in chapter 29, *Life After Earth*.]

The Renewal Power (Easter)

The principle that makes life come from apparent death was/is called **Ausar**, who symbolizes the power of renewal.

Ausar represents the process, growth, and the underlying cyclical aspects of the universe. Therefore, he was also identified with the spirits (energies) of grain, trees, animals, reptiles, birds, etc. The most impressive representation of the concept of regeneration, namely

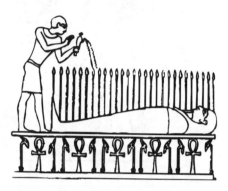

("The Resurrection of the Wheat")

Ausar, is the illustration depicting **Ausar** with 28 stalks of wheat growing out of his coffin. It is also interesting to note that **Ausar**'s life (or his reign), according to the symbolic Egyptian Model Story, lasted 28 (7x4) years.

The Pharaohs, just like the Grand Ancestor **Ausar**, were identified with the crops, and were addressed by titles such as: *Our Crop* and *Our Harvest*.

Ausar's cyclical nature made him relate to the number 7 and its multiples. Very often we find that seven or multiples of seven are needed to account for the principle and sequence of growth. Throughout the entire world, menstruation appears to be connected with the moon, the courses of the moon being likened to the courses of a woman. The moon is thus the appropriate symbol of fertility. As he waxes and wanes, he is regarded as a dying and resurrecting cycle — the symbol of the death and rebirth of the crops. Menstruation in women, on which all human life depends, occurs in a cycle of 28 (7 x 4) days.

Egyptian Kings, like their role model **Ausar**, were regarded as personifications (emanations) of the moon, in addition to the sun. In the cycle of **Ausar-Ra, Ausar** is identified with the moon, the light of the night regions of the dead. **Ausar's** Light is a reflection of **Ra**, in one of his manifestations as the sun.

Ausar died (analogous to the moon's departure) and was resurrected, the third day after that. The third day is the beginning of a new moon, i.e. a renewed **Ausar**. This is reminiscent of the Easter celebration, where, like **Ausar**, the biblical Jesus died on Friday and was resurrected the third day — Sunday — as a new life.

Chapter 18

Auset, The Universal Mother

The Virgin Mother

Auset's (Isis) role in the Egyptian Model Story and the story of the Virgin Mary are strikingly similar, for both were able to conceive without male impregnation. Heru (Horus) was conceived and born after the death of Auset's husband, and, as such, Auset was revered as the Virgin Mother.

Auset is the power responsible for the creation of all living creatures. Ancient Egyptians called her "Auset with the 10,000 names/attributes". Plutarch took note of that and wrote in his *Moralia Vol V,*

> Auset (Isis) is, in fact, the female principle of Nature, and is receptive of every form of generation, in accord with which she is called by Plato the gentle nurse and the all-receptive, and by most people has been called by countless names, since, because of the force of Reason. she turns herself to this thing or that and is receptive of all manner of shapes and forms.

Auset, in Egyptian, means *throne*. [More about the significance of her name in chapter 22.]

Sabt (Sirius), Auset Star

Egypt worked according to an extremely accurate triple calendar. Each calendar had/has its own purpose:

1 - A lunar calendar of alternating 29- and 30-day months.

2 - A civil calendar of 360 days plus five additional days (on which the **neteru** were said to be born).

3 - A calendar of 365 ¼ days based upon the heliacal return of the star **Sabt** (Sirius).

The Egyptians' advanced knowledge in astronomy, as reflected in their calendar, was acknowledged by the great Strabo (64 BCE - 25 CE), who wrote:

"The Egyptian priests are supreme in the science of the sky. Mysterious and reluctant to communicate, they eventually let themselves be persuaded, after much soliciting, to impart some of their precepts; although they conceal the greater part. They revealed to the Greeks the secrets of the full year, whom the latter ignored as with many other things..."

Egypt's ingenious and very accurate calendar was based on the observation and the study of **Sabt's** (Sirius) movements in the sky. The Egyptians regarded **Sabt** as the great central fire, about which our solar system orbits.

During the very remote periods of the Ancient Egyptian history, **Auset** was associated with the star **Sabt** (Sirius), the brightest star in heaven, which was called, like her, the **Great Provider** and whose annual rising ushered in the Nile's inundation and the beginning of the Egyptian Year. It occurred when **Sabt** rose on the horizon together with the sun, and remained visible for a few moments until it faded with the advance of dawn. We refer to this as the *heliacal* (from Greek *helios*, "the sun") rising of **Sabt** (Sirius). This fact is clearly acknowledged in the Webster's dictionary, which defines the Sothic (**Sabt** in Egyptian) year as:

•   *of having to do with Sirius (**Sabt**), the Dog Star*

•   *Designating or of an Ancient Egyptian cycle or period of time based on fixed year of 365 1/4 days (Sothic Year) and equal to 1,460 such years.*

The writing shown here is a memorandum from the Overseer of the temple to the Lector-priest at Nubkaura Temple at el-Lahun (during the time of Senwosret II, 1897-1878 BCE), notifying him that **Sabt** (Sirius) would rise on the 16th day of the 4th month, so as to take note of its exact location and time, and to enter it into the temple records.

The length of the Sothic year was computed from one rising of the Dog Star, **Sabt** (Sirius), to another. But the annual rising of **Sabt** was not the beginning of the year, because **Sabt** appears to move in a spiral orbit, from one year to the next.

For ordinary purposes, such as the dates of their kings and other events, Ancient Egyptians used the civil calendar of the year of 365 days. The civil or moving year gradually shifted in relation to the fixed or Sothic year. Every calculation could thus be corrected, by comparing the time of the list, with that of the Sothic year. The civil year, losing a bit over a day every four years, took 1,461 years to coincide with the Sothic year. The date of this coincidence marked what Egypt called the **New Year**.

Surviving Egyptian records show that the Sothic year was fixed in the year 4240 BCE. There are repeated references in the *Funerary (commonly known as Pyramid) Texts* of the 5th Dynasty Kings (ca. 2500 BCE), referring to a prior inauguration of the **New Year**. Astronomical calculations show that the referenced prior **New Year** occurred in 4240 BCE. We don't know if this was the first time that Egyptians calculated the time of the **New Year**, or if other prior **New Years** occurred in previous Sothic periods. If 4240 BCE was the first recorded **New Year**, the observation and calculation of the differences between the solar and sothic cycles must have started at a much earlier time.

As stated earlier, the beginning of the year was not set at the annual rising of **Sabt** (Sirius), because its path through the heavens has a wavy curve. This is caused by **Sabt's** faint massive companion. **Sabt** and its companion are revolving around their common center of gravity or, in other words, revolving about each other.

Sabt's diameter is less than twice the diameter of our sun. Its companion, however, has a diameter only about three times the diameter of earth, yet it weighs about 250,000 times as much as the earth. Its material is packed together so tightly, that it is about 5,000 times as dense as lead. Such a compression of matter means that **Sabt's** companion's atoms do not exist in their normal states, but are squeezed so closely together, that many atomic nuclei are crowded into a space previously occupied by a single *normal* atom, i.e. the electrons of these atoms are squeezed out of their orbits and move about freely (a degenerate state). This is the Egyptian **Nun**, the *neutron soup* — the origin of all matter and energy in the universe.

The movement of **Sabt's** companion on its own axis, and around **Sabt**, upholds all creation in space, and as such is considered the starting point of creation.

Chapter 19

Set,
The Power of Opposition

The pre-creation state [as described on page 35] was caused by the effect of gravitational/contractional forces that pulled and crushed atoms out of their orbits. The act of creation was/is to bring order to the atoms, by countering/opposing the crushing forces.

Therefore, to the Ancient Egyptians, opposition forces were a necessity of creation and its continuance.

Set

The **neter** (energy/power/force), **Set** (Seth), represents the universal role of opposition.

The world, as we know it — from the smallest particle to the largest planet — is kept in balance by a law that is based on the balanced dual nature of all things. Without the balance between the two opposing forces, there would be no creation, i.e. no universe. For example, the galaxies are mainly subjected to two opposing forces: 1) the *expulsion forces* — resulting from the effect of the *Big Bang* all galaxies moving away from us — and 2) the *gravity forces*, which pull the galaxies together.

Another example (however mundane) is the role of **Set** (opposition) in our ability to walk. The friction of a surface makes it possible to walk, and a lack of friction (like an icy surface) makes it impossible to walk. So, without the opposing resistance of friction, we are unable to walk. Yet, too much friction — the other extreme, such as a thorny surface — also makes it impossible to walk. In other words, resistance, at the proper magnitude, is a necessity in the universe.

It is therefore that **Set** is not *evil* in the narrow sense. He represents the concept of opposition in all aspects of life (physically and metaphysically). Too much or too little of **Set's** powers — or anything else — is not workable. The proper quantity of **Set** — or anything else — is a necessity indeed.

To express the necessity of **Set**, we find the following references in the Ancient Egyptian traditions:

1 - **Set** is one of the Grand Ennead, responsible for the creation of everything. [See chapter 14.]

2 - **Set** symbolizes one of the four elements of solidity/ stability of the universe, namely fire/heat, as mentioned earlier in Plutarch's *Moralia Vol V*,

> *The Egyptians simply give the name of ... Set [Typhon in Greek] ... to all that is dry, fiery, and arid, in general, and antagonistic to moisture.*

3 - **Set** also represents the metaphysical fire/dryness, such as the emotions of love, hate, jealousy, aloofness, anger, temperment, passion, etc, as shown in the *Egyptian Model Story* [chapter 2].
Without fire/heat, the universe cannot exist. Also, being *"antagonistic to moisture"* is essential in the water cycle of evaporation, condensation, ...etc.

At the end of *The Egyptian Model Story*, both **Heru** and **Set** were assigned equal and different roles in the universe [see chapter 2]. **Set** became the ruler of the desert/waste/wilderness areas and their associated animals, such as the immense coiled serpent, the black pig, and the ass. Each animal symbolizes a different aspect of **Set**.

To learn about **Set** is to learn about aspects of ourselves and our universe. The objective is to know how to control and manage these types of **Set** energies.

In the Ancient Egyptian relief shown to the right, **Set** is depicted, guiding the Pharaoh to kill the wicked serpent at the four corners of the world.

Unlike christian theologians, the question of the nature and existence of **Set** gave the Egyptians no trouble at all.

Part

The Universal Replica

Chapter 20

The Human Being

The One Joined Together

For Ancient Egyptians, man, as a miniature universe, represents the created images of all creation. Since **Ra** — the cosmic creative impulse — is called, **The One Join together, Who Comes Out of His Own Members**, so the human being (the image of creation) is likewise, **A One Joined Together**. The human body is a unity that consist of different parts, joined together. In the **Litany of Ra**, the body parts of the divine man are each identified with a **neter/netert**.

If man is the universe in miniature, then all factors in man arc duplicated on a greater scale in the universe. All drives and forces, which are powerful in man, are also powerful in the universe at large. In accordance with the Egyptians' cosmic consciousness, every action performed by man is believed to be linked to a greater pattern in the universe, including sneezing, blinking, spitting, shouting, weeping, dancing, playing, eating, drinking, and sexual intercourse.

Man, to the Ancient Egyptians, was the embodiment of the laws of creation. As such, the physiological functions and processes of the various parts of the body were seen as manifestations of cosmic functions. The limbs and organs had a metaphysical function, in addition to their physical purpose. The parts of the body were consecrated to one of the **neteru** (divine principles), which appeared in the Egyptian records throughout its recovered history.   In addition to the **Litany of Ra**, here are other examples:

• *Utterance 215 § 148-149,* from the Sarcophagus Chamber of Unas' Tomb (rubble pyramid) at Saqqara, identifies the parts of the body (head, nose, teeth, arms, legs, etc), each with the divine **neteru**.

> *Thy head is that of Heru (Horus)*
> *. . .*
> *thy nose is a Anbu (Anubis)*
> *thy teeth are Sopdu*
>
> *thy arms are Happy and Dua-mutef,*
> *. . .*
> *thy legs are Imesty and Kebeh-senuf,*
> *. . .*
> *All thy members are the twins of Atum.*

• From the *Papyrus of Ani,* [pl. 32, item 42]:

> *My hair is Nun; my face is Ra; my eyes are Het-Heru (Hathor); my ears are Wepwawet; my nose is She who presides over her lotus-leaf; my lips are Anbu (Anubis); my molars are Selket; my incisors are Auset (Isis); my arms are the Ram, the Lord of Mendes; my breast is Net (Neith); my back is Set (Seth); my phallus is Ausar (Osiris); . . . my belly and my spine are Sekhmet; my buttocks are the Eye of Heru (Horus); my thighs and my calves are Nut; my feet are Ptah; . . . <u>there is no member of mine devoid of a neter (god)</u>, and Tehuti (Thoth) is the protection of all my flesh.*

The above text leaves no doubt about the divinity of each member:

> <u>*there is no member of mine devoid of a neter (god)*</u>,

The Big Bang — The Divine Parts

The *Big Bang* theory, which sees the creation of the universe as a physical event, was presented thousands of years ago in the Egyptian texts, whereby the Absolute created the universe out of **Nun**, the cosmic ocean. All parts of the universe originated from one source. Since the Origin is Divine, it follows that the parts are also divinized.

The physical event of the Big Bang was transformed into the typical Egyptian story form. This well-crafted Egyptian mystery play was based on the fact that man, as the image of God, represented the created image of all creation. The divinity of the human parts assumed their functions in the storytelling of creation. Here is the sequence of the Big Bang as described in Ancient Egyptian texts.

1 - The first step to start creation, was for the Objective Divine Being (**Atum**) to conceive in his own heart (which is, in cosmic terms, the seat of intellect, mind, conscience) the concept of the multiple (divine beings) out of the One, i.e. the *Big Bang*.
The Ancient Egyptian text, known as the *Bremner-Rhind Papyrus*, **The Book of Knowing the Creations of Ra and Overcoming Apep** (Apophis), states:

> *I conceived in my own heart; there came into being a vast number of forms of divine beings as the forms of children and the forms of their children.*

Creation as a Big Bang resulted in the separation of parts (**children**) and smaller parts (**their children**).

2 - The generation of new beings can only be enacted by the work of two complimentary opposites. The feminine principle of the self-created **Atum** is his hand. [More details later in this chapter.] This was stated in the *Bremner-Rhind Papyrus*:

I it was who aroused desire with my hand.

3 - The build up of the physical forces that caused the *Big Bang* was equated, in human terms, to an erect phallus, and the act of masturbation. Masturbation is the same as the building up of physical forces that led to the *Big Bang*. It's another explanation of the same thing. The Egyptian text in the *Bremner-Rhind Papyrus* states:

I masturbated with my hand.

4 - The created universe was manifested through **Tehuti,** who gave names to the divine beings that resulted from the *Big Bang*. The Egyptian texts state that the created universe came out of the mouth, and the mouth was the symbol of Unity, the One, in hieroglyphs.

The *Bremner-Rhind Papyrus* describes the fiery explosion (*Big Bang*) from the mouth, just like the lava coming out of the volcano's mouth:

I it was who aroused desire with my hand; I masturbated with my hand, I poured out of my mouth. I spat out Shu, I spat out Tefnut.

Atum's children were the twin divine beings, **Shu** and **Tefnut.** As stated earlier, **Shu** and **Tefnut** are the ancestors of all created beings in the universe.

Astrological Personal Maps

The unique individuality of each person was recognized in all aspects of the Ancient Egyptian civilization, such as in medicine. Several Ancient Egyptian medical (mostly categorized as "magical" by academia) papyri were recovered. They belong to different periods and to different localities. These papyri identify the different parts of the patient's body as being under the influence of different **neteru**, and in this way divinized.

In all these Ancient Egyptian medical papyri, the relationships between the divinized parts to particular **neteru** (gods) were different from one person to another. Transformational (funerary) texts were individualized as well. No two "funerary" texts are alike. Therefore, these papyri were personalized astrological maps/charts.

Ancient and Baladi Egyptians' cosmic consciousness led/leads them to the adoption of astrologically-based practices in every aspect of their lives. It is clear that Egyptian medicine had a strong astrological element, as per the following examples:

1 - Egyptians divided the sky into 36 sectors of ten degrees each, called decans. **Ausar,** *The Grand Ancestor,* likewise has 36 forms. Like the sky, the human body, in Ancient Egyptian medicine, was also divided into 36 sectors, and each came under the influence of a certain **neteru/netert** (god/goddess), each controlled by one of the 36 parts of the Egyptian Zodiac. The Egyptian Zodiac consists of 12 months; each month is divided into 3 intervals of 10 days (like decan).

Baladi Egyptians refer to the peculiarities of each of the three intervals of the 30-day month, in all their affairs. It is interesting to note that the "modern" astrological month is also divided into 3 intervals — each with its own peculiar characteristics.

2 - The day, in Egypt, was divided into 12 hours of day
and 12 hours of night. The length of the hour was not
fixed, but varied with the seasons. Long days in the
summer meant longer hours of the day, and the opposite in the winter months. Each hour had its own *influence*. The Egyptian medical papyri advised specific
times at which to administer specific recipes or treat
specific ailments.

3 - The Egyptian physiological system is based on the presence of 12 centers of power. Once, every two hours of
night and day, one or the other of these centers reaches
peak activity, by the passage of **Ra**, the sun of the blood,
and it then returns to sleep. The alterations of the red
and white solar energy to the areas where the twelve
powers lie sleeping within the organs of the body, is
the result of cosmic rhythms. This activity happens
twelve times a day. Twelve is also the number of
months in a year and the number of zodiac signs in the
Great Year.

Acupuncture, which we are told is Chinese, is actually
Egyptian. The Chinese refer to these 12 centers of power,
as *the twelve meridians of the body*.

This Ancient Egyptian belief in the 12 centers was
passed down to the West, in the familiar figure of the medi-
eval astrological man, with his organs and limbs assigned to
the domination of the twelve astrological signs.

[More about the very advanced Egyptian medicine in *Historical Deception: The Untold Story of Ancient Egypt*, by the same
author.]

Metaphysical/Physical Functions of the Parts

It is a human instinct worldwide to use a human organ/part to describe a metaphysical aspect. The Ancient Egyptian texts and symbols are permeated with this complete understanding that the man (whole and parts) is the image of the universe (whole and parts). This understanding was shown earlier, where the *Big Bang* theory was described in human (mini-universe) terms.

Here are a few more examples in Ancient Egypt of the metaphysical/physical functions of some human parts:

* **The Hand**
  The hand symbolized/symbolizes several concepts, one of which is action, and therefore of creation and of latent creative power. As stated earlier, **Atum** created the first beings by copulating with his own hand. **Atum**'s hand personified the female principle inherent within him, and from this union, the divine pair, **Shu** and **Tefnut**, arose. The metaphysical role of the hand is present in texts throughout the known history of Ancient Egypt. Such a concept is found in the *Unas (so-called "Pyramid") Texts* [Spell 1248]. Later, we find it in representational expressions on decorated coffins of the First Intermediate Period (2150-2040 BCE), which depicted the image of the divine couple "**Atum** and his hand." The exact nature of the hand symbolism is seen in the fact that in the New Kingdom (1550-1070 BCE), the title "**neter's** hand" was applied to the wife of **Amen/ Amon** — the legal heiress to the throne. [More about the legal heiress and the matrilineal/matriarchal society in chapter 22.]

  The role of the loving hand found its way into most cultures, for when a man wants to marry, he asks the girl's father for her hand.

- **The Heart**
  The heart was/is considered to be a symbol of intellectual perceptions, consciousness, and moral courage. The heart is symbolized by **Heru** (Horus).

- **The Tongue**
  The tongue is the strongest muscle in the human body. *A man of his word* means *whatever he commands with his tongue will be manifested.* The tongue is symbolized by **Tehuti** (Thoth).

- Both the heart and tongue complement each other, as stated clearly in the Shabaka Stele (716-701 BCE), which is a reproduction from the 3rd Dynasty.

  > *the Heart thinks all that it wishes, and the Tongue delivers all that it wishes.*

  [More about the roles of the heart and tongue in chapter 5.]

- **The Spine and Belly**
  In our modern societies, the guts and spine are symbols of physical courage. This concept has Ancient Egyptian roots. In the **Papyrus of Ani** [pl.32 item 42], we read,

  > *my belly and my spine are Sekhmet*

  Sekhmet is a lioness-headed **netert** (goddess). The lioness is the most fearless animal.

[The metaphysical functions of some other human parts are described through the book.]

Human Measurement Units

The whole metrological system in Egypt was based on the human figure — its units derived from an ideal length of limb. Here are a few examples:

1 - The main standard linear measure was the mh(cubit) : the length of the forearm from elbow to tip of middle finger — further divided into 7 handbreadths/palms of four digits each or 28. One Egyptian cubit is 1.72' or 0.5236m.

2 - In Egypt, the sections of the eye are the glyphs for the fractions $^1/_2$ to $^1/_{64}$, as shown below. Note that the sum of successive division is $^{63}/_{64}$, which will always fall short of unity except at infinity, which is perfectly consistent with Egyptian thought: only the Absolute is One.

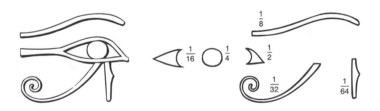

3 - To Egypt, a fraction — any fraction — could only be a fraction of *unity*. Esoterically, because all numbers are to be regarded as divisions of unity, the mathematical relationship a number bears to unity is a key to its nature.

The Ancient Egyptians represented fractions, i.e. having a numerator of 1, by drawing the mouth of **Ra** (shown herein) as the numerator and unit marks underneath for the denominator.

To write $1/7^{\text{th}}$, the Egyptian simply wrote the numeral 7, in an upside-down form, underneath the **mouth of Ra's** symbol. A seventh is called **Ra-Sefhet** = mouth of seven. The glyph might be translated as 'One emits seven'.

In Ancient Egypt, the *words* of **Ra**, revealed through **Tehuti** (equivalent to *Hermes* or *Mercury*), became the parts (fractions) of the world.

[More about fraction mysticism in *Egyptian Harmony: The Visual Music*, by the same author.]

Chapter 21

The Metaphysical Man

The Twin Soul

As stated earlier, Ancient and Baladi Egyptians believe that our earthly existence at the 8th realm (or the first earth) is closely associated with our Siamese twin of the opposite sex, who exists at the 9th realm (also called the 2nd earth/land). Most people, worldwide, usually call this twin the *astral, etheric,* or *spirit* body, a kind of vital image of the body itself. This body is an exact mirror-image replica of our physical body. The astral body at realm 9 has molecules that vibrate at a much faster and higher rate than its physical counterpart. Most people can't see the *astral body*, although Baladi Egyptians, and some people from other cultures, are able to see it psychically.

Several Ancient Egyptian illustrations depict the ram-headed **Khnum** molding two identical twins at the potter's wheel, in affirmation of the concept of the Two Lands/Earths, where the twin souls are subject to the same experiences from date of birth to date of death.

The scene shown below (from a bas-relief in the Temple of Luxor) depicts the twin **neteru, Hapi**, representing the Two Lands/Earths, and bringing forth the twin baby Amenhotep III and his double to **Heru,** who then presents the separated Siamese twins to **Amen-Ra.**

The physical and the *astral* bodies have points of contact. These junctions are known as plexuses. There may be as many as 80,000 in the human body. At the present time, we may only be able to name about 30, and only six or seven are described in any detail.

Plexuses were known to the Ancient Egyptians. From Egypt, the theory spread, by way of the Hellenic world and Byzantium, to the Hesychasts (an order of monks in modern Greece), who distinguish six such plexuses: the forehead, throat, heart, solar plexuses, sex organs and *tail*. Near the human tail is situated one of the most powerful plexuses known to occultism. This important plexus was known to Ancient Egyptians, who portrayed **neteru** with tails.

The Metaphysical Components

According to Ancient and Baladi Egyptian traditions, when the body was born, there came into existence with it an abstract individuality or a spiritual being, which was wholly independent and distinct from the physical body, whose actions it was supposed to direct, and guide, and keep watch over. It lived in the body until the body died.

According to the Egyptians' logic, since the physical body is comprised of various components (chemical, biological, etc), the metaphysical being likewise consists of several metaphysical components — ba, ka, ...etc. The Egyptians dealt with these components in the same manner as our modern chemistry deals with the chemical elements and compounds of oxygen, hydrogen, carbon, ...etc.

The major metaphysical components are:

- The **ba** is immortal. When the **ba** departs, the body dies. The **ba** is represented as a human-headed bird, which is the opposite of the normal depiction of **neteru** (gods) as human bodies  with animal heads — in other words, as the divine aspect of the terrestrial. The **ba** may be shown as a stork, or as a falcon. The stork is known for its migrating and homing instinct. The stork is known worldwide as the bird who carries newborn babies to their new families. The stork returns to its own nest with consistent precision, hence a migratory bird, par excellence, is the bird chosen for the *soul*. **Ba** is usually translated as *soul*.

- The **ka** is the combination of several inter-
  twined subcomponents. It is equated to
  what we describe as *personality*. The **ka** does
  not die with the mortal body, although it
  may break into its many subcomponents.
  The **ka** is portrayed as a pair of arms out-
  stretched towards heaven.

- The **khaibit** seems to correspond with our notion of the
  ghost.

- The **khu** is a higher spiritual element. It is a shining
  and luminous component. **Khu-s** are also heavenly beings, living with the **neteru** (gods). Each **khu** may then
  be equivalent to the *guardian angel*.

- The **akh** is the beneficient *spirit* gained through piety
  and good deeds.

- The **ab** is the heart, which corresponds to *conscience*.

- The **sekhem** is the personification of the *inner strength*
  of a man.

Part

Social Harmony

Chapter 22

Social & Political Structures

The Aminated Society

Herodotus, in 500 BCE stated; *"of all the nations of the world, Egyptians are the happiest, healthiest, and most religious"*. These are the three elements — happy, healthy, and religious — of the ideal society. The reason for such an ideal society is their total cosmic consciousness.

What we consider to be a "political" structure, was for them a natural aspect of their social structure. In order to achieve perfect universal harmony, the social structure must mirror the same orderly hierarchy of the created universe. Human survival and success require that the same orderly structure be maintained. *As above so below* is the only way to achieve order and harmony.

Their cosmic awareness was/is transformed into traditions and proverbs. Everybody knows what to do — one for all and all for one.

Harmonic Matrilineal/Matriarchal Society

The Ancient Egyptians were totally aware of the planetary laws. The modern "discovery"/rediscovery of such laws are attributed to Johannes Kepler (1571-1630), who himself boasted in print that he had rediscovered the lost laws of Egypt. [See page 135.] He was honest, but his followers were/are not.

Kepler rediscovered that the orbit of a planet/comet about its sun is an egg-shaped path (ellipse). Each planetary system is balanced only when the planet's orbit is an egg-shaped plane that has 2 focci, with its sun's center of mass at one of its focci.

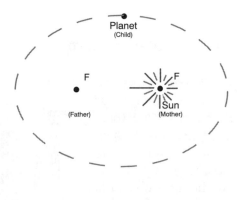

The creation stories in Ancient Egypt begin with the *cosmic egg* (an elliptical shape). In the **Khmunu** (Hermopolis) traditions, the *cosmic egg* contained the *bird of light* (the sun). All planets/comets follow the egg-shaped (elliptical) orbit, with a sun at one of its focci.

Likewise, on earth, the female is the source of energy — the sun. It is her power that keeps the children (planets), each in its own independent orbit. That is to say, the matrilineal/matriarchal system follows the planetary laws.

The matriarchal system, as the social manifestation of planetary laws, was the basis of the social organization in Ancient Egypt, where the queen sister and queen mother had positions of great respect and potentially much authority.

Throughout Egyptian history, it was the queen who transmitted the solar blood. The queen was the true sovereign, landowner, keeper of the royalty, and guardian of the purity of the lineage. Egyptian Kings claimed a right to the throne through marriage with the eldest Egyptian princess. Through marriage, she transmitted the crown to her husband, he only acted as her executive agent. This social/political law was reflected in the Egyptian folklore of **Ausar**, who became the first Pharaoh of Egypt, as a result of his marrying **Auset**. **Auset** means *seat*, i.e. *authority*. **Auset** is the principle of legitimacy — the actual physical throne.

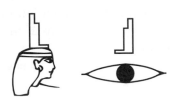

As a rule, in the Egyptian tombs as far back as the Old Kingdom, the mother of the deceased is represented with the wife, while the father rarely appears. On the funerary stelae of later times also, it is the usual custom to trace the descent of the deceased on the mother's side, and not on that of the father. The person's mother is specified, but not the father, or he is only mentioned incidentally.

Surviving records from the Middle Kingdom (2040-1783 BCE) show that the nomes (provinces) of Egypt passed from one family to another through heiresses; thus he who married the heiress would govern the province.

Western academicians are uncomfortable with writing about the matrilineal and matriarchal societies. Some even went so far as to state that the reason they traced the mothers only, was because fathers were unknown or in doubt. They are in pain, trying to deny, ignore, downplay, and explain it through their own dark sides. Their underlying, pathetic, resentful and contemptuous thinking is, ***what Europe did not have, cannot be!***

Polity/Nome

A polity is like a small stellar system that revolves around a common purpose. A polity usually consists of a number of extended families living in compounds clustered within a narrow area, or scattered about in groups. Each family has a specialty in which it excels, and between the neighboring family lineages, the different tasks are harmoniously divided.

Each family lineage (called *Ginne*, and meaning *ancestor*) consists of a number of family units who share the same female line. A common Egyptian Baladi proverb goes, *a maternal uncle is [like] a father*, emphasizing the genetic female lineage.

Each family has a leader, or family head, who is responsible for the material and spiritual welfare of every member of the family lineage. He also maintains law, order, justice, and harmony. The elders settle internal disputes among their family members.

Members of the same family lineage cannot marry, except in special well-defined cases that avoid genetic weakening of the family lineage. Incest for them is much more than marriage between siblings or first cousins.

The polity's political structure is truly a grassroot democracy, with the proper representation. A council of respected elders, from the established lineages of the community, elects and assists the leader in the governance of the community. The council serves as a court, helps the leader allocate access to resources, carries out rituals, and organizes public works.

Other polity's offices include that of village spiritual intermediary, which may be different from the leader. The spiritual intermediary links the community ritually to the authority of the local spirits of the land and the spirits of past leaders whose aid and retributions he interprets.

Commonwealth Alliance of Polities

The needs of a civilized society cannot be fully satisfied by the produce of its village polity. In order to protect the individuality of the polity and its socio-political effectiveness, a co-op system between several polities is needed. In other words, a large society should be like a galaxy composed of several planetary groups. No planetary group dominates another. They are all independent groups that harmonize about common interests. On earth, this would be the commonwealth-type alliance.

Unlike the autocratic centralized-type government, the form of a commonwealth-type government recognizes the importance of the grassroots — local communities. Coalitions are formed to share specific duties and responsibilities that can benefit all of them.

The cooperative polities are represented by each's leader, to form a council of elders/leaders. There are several ways to run such an alliance:

1 - The council elects a local leader to be recognized as a leader of a group of polities.
2 - The council elects a rotating leader.
3 - Commonwealth(s) may find and choose a spiritual leader, like a Pharaoh whose main duty was to supplicate spirits of the land to renew its fertility, and to engage the help of chiefly ancestors to foster the welfare of the land and people.
[More about the role of the Pharaoh in chapter 24.]

Alliances can be resolved, changed or restructured, and they did so throughout the Ancient Egyptian history. We should not misunderstand this to mean upheaval, but the true application of *Live and Let Live*. This is a true grassroots democracy.

Central-Type Government Failings

A central-type government, notwithstanding their self-proclaimed superiority, is not *of the people, by the people, for the people*. Their emphasis on "individuality" — as far as one man, one vote — is a misrepresentation of the society. Breaking up the society into individuals produces a socially (as well as economically and politically) chaotic society. It is a system based on patronizing the individual and convincing him/her that s/he is truly represented by a politician who will say anything to be elected. The reality is that enacting laws in these broken societies is based on the power of the special interest groups, and individual voters have no power.

In the grassroot democratic commonwealth system, the elders of family groups are the true and honest representatives. In other words, these elders represent a true "interest group" — their families, trades, and community.

The central-type government is the cause and effect of the social upheaval. The government became a *substitute family*, providing social benefits. In the process, they impose (legalized or otherwise) taxes, collect them, and re-distribute them again (kind of)! This is an autocratic and not a democratic system, where many layers of bureaucracy are formed, whose main interest is the self-preservation of their jobs. In the process, they complicate people's lives. The central government's response is to use force (tax collectors, police, military, etc), more bureaucracy and more autocracy in the name of "enforcing the laws".

The only equitable, harmonic, and efficient system is the commonwealth-type government.

Chapter 23

Division of Labor

Work Ethics

The Ancient Egyptian tombs portray daily life activities in the presence of the **neteru** or with their assistance, signifying the importance of active work as a prerequisite to be admitted into higher heavenly realms. The whole **42 Negative Confessions** that one must adhere to are about work performance and work ethics, such as:

I have not laid waste the ploughed land.

Ancient and Baladi Egyptians are identified by their work. The person's family name was/is the family's profession/trade (Carpenter, Smith, Farmer, Taylor, ...etc.). Work is honorable, as per an instruction from an Ancient Egyptian papyrus:

Be industrious, an idle man is not honorable.

Most references in Ancient Egypt were to farming, which is/was the main, but not the only, occupation. Farming, however, provides the best metaphors for our earthly purpose — to nourish the seed within — such as the powerful symbolism of: *One reaps what one sows.*

Inborn Destiny (Genetic History)

The Ancient and Baladi Egyptian societies are divided into various labor groups. To some extent, an individual's labor group is determined by birth. Ancient Egypt, did not have castes, in the strictest sense of the word, but the various groups recognized the inborn genetic qualities in a family lineage.

Heredity is important in determining most people's destinies. A common expression, "nature vs. nurture", raises the eternal question — how much is inborn, and how much is a result of our upbringing/environment.

It would take several generations to acquire the knack or the special skills peculiar to a given type of job. Relying on habit, the sense of custom and tradition, Egyptians generally preferred to stay within the confines of the profession in which they had been raised — the ancestral profession — for their own personal good and for that of society as a whole.

Though a son usually followed the profession of his father, owing to habit, thoughts, education, or patronage and connection, which have existed at all times and in all countries, he could still enter a different profession/trade, but could only perform the less complicated tasks.

The Egyptian system allows the building up of work experience at an early age. The inborn skills, together with such acquisition of experience, are much more efficient and productive than our present-day broken societies.

In our post-Industrial Revolution societies, we waste time and energy in state-mandated schooling. Most people don't become effective in their trade/profession until they are about 30 years old. To be born into a trade/profession, one would be able to contribute at a much earlier age.

The Various Divisions

There was a general division of labor into five main groups:

1 - Intermediaries, consisting of the clergy at the temples and shrines, judges, and doctors.

2 - The farming community, consisting of nobles, farmers, stock breeders, gardeners, supervisors of waterway activities and duties (such as irrigation, water and fishing rights, etc.), huntsmen, boatmen, traders, and shopkeepers.

3 - Specialized professionals (artisans), consisting of the energy handlers, such as: the smiths, leatherworkers, woodworkers, weavers and bards (wordsmiths), as well as masons, and probably potters.

4 - Servile bondsmen, usually serving a long-term contract. These are not slaves at all.

5 - This last group mainly consists of people without a permanent home address, such as the herdsmen groups, pastors, oxherds, shepherds, goatherds, swineherds, poulterers, and fowlers.

[More details about these groups can be found in *Exiled Egyptians: The Heart of Africa*, by same author.]

Intermarriage between the various work groups does not normally take place (but is/was not forbidden or discouraged), not because of a lack of respect between the various divisions — this is not a racist or cultural superiority complex. It is meant to maximize the knowledge, by maintaining the talent of each ancestral lineage, and not to scatter or dilute it.

Chapter 24

The Cosmic Link

The Eternal Power

As per the Ancient Egyptian commonwealth system, the Pharaohs and chiefs had no political power — their main function was to act as intermediaries between the natural and supernatural worlds, by conducting rites and sacrifices. They were not expected to be leaders of victorious armies, but were expected to secure a regular succession of rich harvests. They were identified with the crops, and were addressed as: *Our Crop* and *Our Harvest*.

Based on his extensive training with the powers of the supernatural, the Pharaoh's body was believed to be charged with a divine dynamism that communicated itself to everything he touched. Diodorus reported that the Pharaoh typically led a restricted life. Not even the most intimate of his courtiers might see him eat or drink. When the King ate, he did so in private. The food was offered to him with the same ritual as was used by priests in offering sacrifice to the **neteru** (gods).

The authority of a leader/King, and his legitimacy to

rule over his people, were derived from his acceptance by his subjects as the descendant of the founding ancestor of the people. He was, in essence, the cosmic link between the present and the past.

According to the Ancient Egyptian Model [chapter 2], the present is **Heru** (Horus), who came out of the past — **Ausar** (Osiris). This is eloquently illustrated in the **Ausar** Temple at **Abtu** (Abydos), as shown below, whereby **Heru** is being born out of **Ausar**, after his death.

Accordingly, all the Pharaohs identified themselves with **Heru** (Horus) as a living King, and with the soul of **Ausar** (Osiris) as a dead King. The right to rule was considered to be a continuous chain of legitimacy, which was based on the matriarchal principles [as explained in chapter 22].

The eternal power of the leader/King never dies. The power is merely transferred from one human body to another human body (medium).

Even the British of today follow, unconsciously, the same belief that the eternal power transfers from one human body to another, when they say, *"The king is dead. Long live the king."* As if to say **Ausar** *is dead. Long live* **Heru**.

The Master Servant

The Ancient Egyptian King, with the help of the priests associated with him, via the ancestral spirits, established a proper relationship between the people and the supernatural forces. The leader was regarded as having a personal influence over the works of nature, to whom divine honors were paid and to whom divine powers were attributed.

The Ancient Egyptian Pharaoh was an earthly image of the sum of divine energies of the universe (**neteru**). As such, he continually performed the necessary rituals for proper relationship and communication with the **neteru** (the powers of the universe), in order to maintain the welfare of the state, and to insure the fertility of the earth, that it may bring forth sustenance. Each year, the King hoed the first plot of farming land and sowed the first seeds. If the Pharaoh did not perform the daily liturgy to the **neteru**, the crops would perish. He spent his time performing his duties to his people, by performing the necessary rituals, from one temple to another throughout the whole country.

Despite the repeated charges of vanity against the Pharaohs, it is worth remembering that their abodes while on earth were never made of stone, but of mud-brick, the same material used by the humblest peasants. These humble mortal monarchs believed that the impermanent body, formed of clay by **Khnum**, the ram-headed **neter**, called for an equally impermanent abode on this earth. The earthly houses of the Kings have long since returned to the earth from which they were raised.

Keeping The Flame Alive

The fertility of the soil, the abundant harvests, the health of people and cattle, the normal flow of events and all phenomena of life, were/are intimately linked to the potential of the ruler's vital force.

The Egyptian King was not supposed (or even able) to reign unless he was in good health and spirit. Accordingly, he was obliged to rejuvenate his vital force, by regularly attending physical and metaphysical practices, which are known as the **Heb-Sed** rituals.

One of the **Heb-Sed** rituals was to induce a near death experience, so that the King could travel in the higher realms, to rejuvenate his cosmic powers. When he returned back, he would be a "new" King. More meaning to the phrase: *The King is dead — Long Live the King.*

Chapter 25

Interacting With Energies

The Physical/Metaphysical Society

The Ancient and Baladi Egyptians made/make no distinction between a metaphysical state of being and one with a material body. Such a distinction is a mental illusion, as accepted now in scientific circles, since Einstein's relativity theory — that matter is a form of energy.

The universal energy matrix — according to the Egyptian traditions — consists of the unity of nine (7 heavens and 2 lands) inter-penetrating and interactive realms. As such, Ancient and Baladi Egyptians maintained/maintain communications between their earthly realm and their ancestral spirits and **neteru** (gods), in the other realms.

The most common communications were/are between earthly beings and their ancestor spirits, who inhabit the first higher/heavenly realm (the one nearest Earth). The spirits (energies) of the departed are supposed to mingle freely with the living, in their earthly journeys. The departed spirits convey warnings, encouragement, direction, and admonitions to human beings through various means, such as in dreams, or through subtle communications via birds, animals, a candle flicker, ...etc.

The interactions with the other non-earthly realms were/are achieved via specialized intermediaries.

The Intermediaries

In order to have peace, stability, good health, and prosperity, it is necessary to stay in harmony with nature. Antisocial acts or bad luck signal that this harmony has been upset, thereby requiring efforts to restore it through ritual acts, such as sacrifices, libations, communions, dances, and symbolic struggles. It is therefore important to determine who or what is responsible for any disorder. Trained intermediaries are employed to rectify these disorders and imbalances, by interpreting spiritual forces, and providing the means to influence them.

1 - **On the cosmic level** — The priesthood at the large temples were/are the officially delegated subordinates of the King. They perform the necessary rituals to ensure the well-being of the land and people. These large temples were built as shrines for the **neteru** (the divine aspects/forces of the universe). Any equilibrium between the mass of humanity and the divine aspects are thus maintained by the Pharaoh/leader and the priesthood. [More about the role of the Pharaoh/leader in chapter 24.]

2 - **On a societal level** — The chief of every large village, town, or district, usually attaches/attached a man to his service, who was believed to be able to hold communication with the ancestor spirits and to have influence with them. This person was also believed to possess powers of an occult character with which, when necessary, he could control, limit, or abrogate the action of evil spirits.

Two common terms, "magic" and "sorcery", both represent the ability to influence life forces. From society's standpoint, "magic" is positive or neutral. On the one hand, "magicians" try to influence life forces to alter the physical world, perhaps to bring good fortune or a return to health. "Sorcerers", on the other hand, are antisocial, using sorcery to control or consume the vital force of others. Unlike "magicians", whose identity is generally known, sorcerers hide their supernatural powers, practicing their rites in secret.

When misfortune occurs, people often suspect that sorcery is at the root of their troubles. They seek counsel from "diviners" or "magicians" to identify the source of the problem, and to help to rectify the situation. If the disruption is deemed to threaten everyone, leaders may act on behalf of the community at large to counterbalance the negative forces. In the process, no individuals are prosecuted, condemned, or punished. This is unlike the common christian and moslem *witch hunts*, whose real goal is to prosecute the non-believers of their dogmas.

3 -   **On an individual level** — Special practitioners in Ancient and Baladi Egypt dealt/deal with everyday life disorders such as: misfortune, sickness, infertility, drought, famine, floods, political rivalries, inheritance disputes, marital or career choices, etc.

If it is thought that an "evil spirit" has possessed a person, the "diviner" or "magician" may take care of it, or an exorcist with a greater degree of specialization may be called in.

These special practitioners (*medicine men*) are the ones who dispense and activate the inner powers of charms, bags full of fetishes, and medicinal products, prior to their use. [More about such items at end of this chapter.]

The Cosmic Shrines (Temples)

The Egyptian temples were not built for public worship, but as shrines for the **neteru** (gods, goddesses), who represent the different powers of the One God. The temple is the link, the proportional mean, between the Macrocosmos (world) and Microcosmos (man). It was a stage on which meetings were enacted between the **neter/netert** (god/goddess) and the King, as a representative of the people.

The Egyptian temple was a machine for maintaining and developing divine energy. It was the place in which the cosmic energy, **neter/netert** (god/goddess), came to dwell and radiate its energy to the land and people.

Only after the **neteru** (gods) had examined the temple destined for them, did they come and dwell there, as clearly stated in this Ancient Egyptian text:

> *'When the great winged scarab rises from the primordial ocean and sails through the heavens in the guise of Heru [Horus] . . .he stops in the heaven before this temple and his heart is filled with joy as he looks at it. Then he becomes one with his image, in his favorite place . . .. he is satisfied with the shrine that the king . . . has erected for him.'*

The walls of the Egyptian temple were covered with animated images — including hieroglyphs — to facilitate the communication between the Above and the Below.

Understanding this function helps us to regard Egyptian art as something vital and alive. Therefore, we must forego viewing the temple as an interplay of forms against a vague historical, archeological presentation. Instead, we must try to see it as the relationship between form and function.

The harmonious power of the temple plans, the images engraved on the walls, and the forms of worship — all led to the same goal; a goal that was both spiritual, as it involved setting superhuman forces in motion, and practical, in that the final awaited result was the maintenance of the country's prosperity.

The temple's rituals were based upon and coordinated with the movements of the heavens, which were in turn manifestations of divine cosmic law. The temple's rituals included, among other things, presenting material offerings: bread, beer, rolls of linen, meat, fowl, and other goods.

Offerings are the fruit of the Egyptians' labor, literally and figuratively — the transformed products of raw material. The **neteru** did likewise — transforming **Nun** into orderly creation. The Egyptian view was that all mundane activities were resonant with the cosmic process of transforming raw matters into perfected creations.

The natures of material objects were transmuted into spirit entities when they were laid upon consecrated altars. The character of the Egyptian offering is shown by the common word for offering, **hetep**, which means *a gift of peace*, or *propitiation*. The stone or wooden tablet on which the offerings were laid is also called **hetep**. The altar was believed to possess the power of transmuting the offerings that were laid upon it, and of turning them into spiritual entities of such a nature that they became suitable "food" for the **neteru**/spirits. In other words, the **neteru** consume only the spirits, or "doubles", of the bread, beer, vegetables, meat, oil, etc. [More about offerings on pg 131.]

[More information about the design and construction of the temples is in *Egyptian Harmony: The Visual Music*, by same author. Other information about temples are provided in *Historical Deception: The Untold Story of Ancient Egypt*, and *Egypt: A Practical Guide*, by the same author.]

Shrines of Wali-s (Shepherds/Saints)

As stated on page 64, beings from higher realms descend to the earthly realm as human beings, to aid and assist others. These people are considered to be gifts from God, and are called Wali-s (caretakers, shepherds). When they are in their earthly realm, they show signs of supernatural powers. They are the intermediaries between the earthly living beings and the supernatural, heavenly realms.

After these Wali-s leave earth, people continue to communicate with them. Each Wali conveys to the earthly living beings a location for a meeting place — a shrine. As a result, a shrine is set apart for him/her, which is tended and kept clean by his/her descendants, free of charge for visitors. Such shrines, in most cases, are not their tombs. These shrines dot the Egyptian landscape since its earliest known history.

Ancient and Baladi Egyptians stayed/stay in touch with the Wali-s. People regularly visit the Wali-s — at their shrines — from surrounding communities. It is a social obligation to visit them, especially on his/her *mou-led* (birthday). Ancient and Baladi Egyptians attend such *mouleds* of Walis, all over Egypt. The official annual number of *mouleds* is estimated at more than 3,000 (1998).

In addition to visitations, people may also ask these Wali-s for personal favors. Vows are made by individuals that if the Wali resolves a personal concern, the vower will donate certain items for charity.

Unlike the christian saints, Wali-s are chosen by ordinary people based on performance. Once the people can see that this person does indeed have the ability to influence supernatural forces, in order to assist those on earth, and as a result fulfills their wishes, then s/he is recognized as a Wali.

Visiting Family's Ancestors

In concurrence with the universal energy matrix, departed ancestors inhabit in the first heaven/realm, nearest to the earthly realm. They connect these two worlds specifically by linking earthly lineage members with their earliest forebears. Because of their proximity, and because they once walked the earth, ancestors are prone to intervene in daily affairs. This intervention is particularly likely in the case of individuals who did not make it to the next realm and are "stuck" in limbo between the earthly and heavenly realms. In such a case, special rituals are made to encourage these spirits to take their leave with serenity.

As there is no distinction between the physical (earthly) and metaphysical society, departed family members are regularly visited (once a week), as a social obligation by their earthly relatives. Ancient and Baladi Egyptians had/have no problem communicating with their departed relatives.

Trees, as part of the animated universe, act as a convenient medium between the earthly and departed souls. The Egyptian term for *sacred grove*, is **Ginne-na** / **Guinea-na**, meaning *the place of ancestor spirits*. If a **gin** (ancestor) tree — a tree with a spirit living in it — is nearby, people often write notes and attach them to the branches of the tree.

Wise men and women consult departed spirits constantly, and periodically spend several days with them at the *spirited grove*.

The Physical/Metaphysical Offerings

The energy matrix of the physical body will disintegrate — weaken and ultimately die — if it is not provided with food and drink. Likewise, a departed spirit (energy matrix) requires sustenance; otherwise it will disintegrate, decompose, or convert into other forms of energies. In simple terms, departed souls are always hungry and thirsty, and so must be supplied with food and drink.

As stated on page 128, the spirits/energies of the higher realms only consume the *spirit* of the offerings.

The Ancient and Baladi Egyptians made offerings to the spirits of their ancestors, with the intention of keeping their help and protection by maintaining their existence. Their existence was finite, and appears to have terminated whenever funerary offerings failed to be made to them on a regular basis. Neglect would cause them to lose their force that helped those still living on earth.

Animal sacrifice was/is the main method to communicate with the metaphysical energies/spirits. Ancient and Baladi Egyptians ate/eat the meat of the sacrificed animals, so as to be blessed by the supernatural forces who consume the *spirit* of these animals. Eating meat was/is not considered to be a part of their standard diet.

Bad spirits are also offered sacrifices to appease them, when some evil has befallen the family. The powers of evil/mischievous spirits were believed to be greater than while on earth, for their freedom from the body gave them greater ability to do harm to people. This action is in concurrence with the common saying, *"Give the devil its due!"*

Dwellings for the Wandering Spirits

As stated earlier, the spirit/energy matrix that animated the human flesh/matter at birth, and left the body (matter) at death, can likewise reside in any other matter, for as long as it wants to. In order to communicate with a departed (free) spirit, a dwelling place — a condensed form of energy, possibly matter — is needed, in order for the free spirit to manifest and communicate its will and influence to the living beings on earth. **Neteru** and ancestral spirits possessed places in which to dwell, and they were believed to enter and leave their statues at will. Therefore, the Ancient and Baladi Egyptians provide dwelling places for spirits of all kinds, in the form of statues and amulets.

- **Statues** — Statues and effigies in temples served as dwelling places for the **neteru**/cosmic energies. These statues were carefully designed to match each **neter's** exact replica.

    A passage from the stele of King Neferhotep (5,000 years ago) at **Abtu** (Abydos), describes his plan to seek original information from the archives, about the exact traditional form of the statue of **Ausar** (Osiris):

    > I will fashion [him, his limbs-his face, his fingers] according to that which my person has seen in the rolls of his [forms].

The Egyptians also prepared a figure or statue of the deceased person, taking great pains to give it all the characteristics of the deceased, so that the **ka** might recognize it as an image of its body and be pleased to enter into the figure and take up its abode there. These figures or statues were placed in the tomb with the body.

- **Amulets** — Amulets are/were used to provide their us-
  ers with certain powers, mostly for protection from evil
  spirits. The Egyptians wore amulets of all kinds when
  living, and placed amulets on bodies of the dead because it was thought that the benevolent, in-dwelling
  spirits would protect them from the evil spirits. The
  tombs of Egypt have yielded untold thousands of beads
  of all kinds, shells, teeth of animals and men, pendants,
  etc., which could be worn as necklaces. The same practice continues with Baladi Egyptians.

For those who could not afford a properly made stone
or metal amulet, it was sufficient if a man were pro-
tected by a drawing of the amulet and a written copy of
the words that were associated with it. Thus, in the
Book of the Coming Forth By Light, we have pictures of
several amulets, each accompanied by its formula.

Neither the Ancient Egyptian nor their Baladi descendants believed in the divinity of their amulets or fetishes, and they never considered them to represent
deities. These objects are simply local residences. A
spirit (energy matrix) can live anywhere, and in anything. The thing itself, the material itself, is nothing
more than a medium. The user makes a clear distinction between a certain material object and the spirit,
for the time inhabiting it. For this reason, nothing is
too small, or too ridiculous, to be considered fit for a
spirit's local residence. For when the spirit is supposed
to have gone out of that thing, i.e. vacate it, and defi-
nitely abandons it, the object itself is discarded/thrown
away as useless.

Chapter 26

Tuning To the Universe

Astronomical Consciousness

Egypt, recognizing the influence of the heavens on earth, observed the skies with the utmost attention. The data of astronomy was studied for its meaning: that is to say, the study of correspondences between events in the heavens and events on earth. Astronomy and astrology were, for them, two sides of the same coin.

A systematic kind of astronomical observation began in very early times. The most ancient astronomical texts, presently known, are found on the lids of wooden coffins dating from the 9th Dynasty (c. 2150 BCE). These texts are called 'diagonal calendars' or 'diagonal star clocks'. They give the names of the decans (stars which rose at ten-day intervals at the same time as the sun), of which there were 36. More elaborate star charts were found in the New Kingdom (1550-1070 BCE) on the ceiling of the tomb of Senenmut, Queen Hatshepsut's architect, and on the ceiling at the temple of Abtu (Abydos). In the tombs of Ramses IV, VII, and IX, inscriptions that relate to the first and the 16th day of each month, give the position occupied by a star at each of the 12 hours of the night in relation to a seated figure: 'over the left ear', 'over the right ear', etc.

While Western academia accredits knowledge of astronomy to the Greeks, early historians reported otherwise. The great Strabo (64 BCE - 25 CE) admitted that:

> *"The Egyptian priests are supreme in the science of the sky...[the Egyptians]...impart some of their precepts; although they conceal the greater part. [The Egyptians] revealed to the Greeks the secrets of the full year, whom the latter ignored as with many other things..."*

"Modern" astronomy is accredited to the works of Johannes Kepler (1571-1630 CE), and that he "discovered" the three planetary laws:

Law 1. The orbit of a planet/comet about the sun is an ellipse with the sun's center of mass at one focus.

Law 2. A line joining a planet/comet and the sun sweeps out equal areas in equal intervals of time.

Law 3. The squares of the periods of the planets are proportional to the cubes of their semi-major axes.

Yet none of these Western academicians tell us how Kepler arrived (out of thin air) at these conclusions. In truth, Kepler boasted in print, at the end of *Book V* of his series, *Harmony of the World*, that he rediscovered the lost laws of Egypt, as stated below:

> *"Now, eighteen months after the first light, three months after the true day, but a very few days after the pure Sun of that most wonderful study began to shine, nothing restrains me; <u>it is my pleasure to yield to the inspired frenzy, it is my pleasure to taunt mortal men with the candid acknowledgment that I am stealing the golden vessels of the Egyptians to build a tabernacle to my God from them, far, far away from the boundaries of Egypt."</u>*

The jubilant Kepler did not state that he himself discovered anything. Rather it was all Ancient Egyptian.

The Earth's Wobble and the Zodiac Ages

Let us review the cause of the zodiac ages. The moon and the sun both tug, gravitationally, on the equatorial bulge of our earth. The moon tries to get the bulge into the plane of its orbit around the earth, and the sun tries to get this bulge into the plane of the earth's orbit around the sun. As a result, the earth does not spin true upon its axis: but more like a slightly off-center spinning top. The combined result of these two tendencies causes the axis of the Earth to make a double cone in space, centered on the center of Earth. This motion is called *precession*.

If the sky is regarded as a constellated backdrop, then because of the *wobble* of the earth upon its axis, the vernal equinox each year rises against a gradually shifting background of constellations. Astronomers call this the *precession of the equinoxes*.

The precession of the equinoxes, through the constellations, gives names to the various twelve zodiac ages. It takes roughly 2,160 years for the equinox to precess through a zodiac sign. Thus it takes some 25,920 years for the spring equinox to traverse the full circuit of the constellations of the twelve zodiac signs. This complete cycle is called the Great Year.

Western academia disregarded the overwhelming physical evidence, as well as the affirmation of ancient sources, that the precession of the equinoxes was known in Egypt, since its recovered archeological findings (5,000 years ago). Academia handed the credit to the Greek Hipparchus of the 2nd century BCE. They never tell us how he arrived at such phenomena out of thin air. Kepler told us, honestly, *"with the candid acknowledgment that I am stealing the golden vessels of the Egyptians to build a tabernacle to my God from them, far, far away from the boundaries of Egypt."*

The Zodiac Constellation of Ancient Egypt

The zodiac constellation of Ancient Egypt is shown at the **Het-Heru** (Hathor) Temple at Dendera. It is clearly Ancient Egyptian, with its figures, symbols, etc.

The Zodiac Constellation in Ancient Egypt

Even though this temple, like a few other Ancient Egyptian temples, was restored during the Greco-Roman period, they were all rebuilt according to Ancient Egyptian plans and symbols.

The texts inscribed in the crypts of the temple of **Het-Heru** at Dendera clearly state that the temple that was restored during the Ptolemaic Era was based on drawings dating back to King Pepi of the 6ᵗʰ Dynasty (2400 BCE). The drawings themselves are copies of pre-dynastic documents. The text reads:

> *"The venerable foundation in Dendera was found in early writings, written on a leather roll in the time of the Servants of Heru (= the kings preceding Mena/ Menes), at Men-Nefer [Memphis], in a casket, at the time of the lord of the Two Lands... Pepi."*

Affirmation of the Egyptian knowledge of the zodiac ages came from Herodotus. He reported that Egyptian priests informed him that the sun had twice set where it now rose, and twice risen where it now set. The statement refers to the progressional cycles of the equinox. The progression results in the rising against a different sign of the Zodiac approximately every two thousand years.

In Rhythm with the Zodiac Ages

There is strong evidence throughout Egypt that the zodiac was known, and was implemented in their works, at least as far back as the Age of Leo (the Lion). A single historical piece of evidence — the Sphinx (a lion with human head) may be that physical evidence.

Egypt responded to the different zodiac ages by applying different means and modes of expression for each zodiac age, which were based upon the inherent specific nature of each age. The applications included items, such as the character of buildings, artwork, names, ...etc.

The Age of Taurus (The Bull)

About 4000 BCE, the symbolism of **Mentu**, the bull, became the most predominant feature of Egyptian art.

Many of the Kings of the Old Kingdom incorporated **Mentu** in their names.

The Age of Taurus (**Mentu** the Bull) ended with the Pharaohs Mentuhoteps I to V. In the Temple of **Mentu** dedicated to **Mentu**hotep II, the King is shown as an old man. This is contrary to the Egyptian practice of depicting the Pharaohs in the prime of their

Mentu, the Bull

life. The depiction of **Mentu**hotep II as an old man, signified the end of the Age of Taurus, the Bull.

The Age of Aries (The Ram)

When the Age of Aries (the Ram) arrived (about 2000 BCE), the Egyptian records revealed the new Age. **Mentu** the bull disappeared, and was succeeded by the ram of **Amen/Amon/ Amun**. **Amen** rose to eminence with his ram-headed symbol.

Ram-headed figures dominated the Egyptian buildings. Ram-headed sphinxes were aligned at the entrance of the Karnak Temple, dedicated to **Amen**. The Pharaohs incorporate **Amen** in the names they assumed: **Amen**hotep, Tutankh**amen**, etc.

Additional confirmation of the ram-headed **Amen** and its symbolism during the Age of Aries, is found in the Triple Shrine of **Amen/Mut/Khonsu**, at the Karnak Temple. On the left wall, **Amen/Amon/ Amun** is pictured as a ram, traveling across the heavens on his barge. This representation, together with the references in many texts to **Amen** as a ram in the sky, support the astronomical/astrological significance.

Some people invented, without any evidence whatsoever, a priestly power struggle at around 2000 BCE, and the result was the victory of **Amen's** priests. There is absolutely no evidence of priestly warfare during the history of Ancient Egypt, except with the 'apparent' case of Akhenaton.

[More about his story is told in *Historical Deception: The Untold Story of Ancient Egypt* and *Tut-Ankh-Amen: The Living Image of the Lord,* by this same author.]

Part

The Earthly Voyage

Chapter 27

Our Purpose on Earth

Sound Reunification

The essence of the Egyptian metaphysical beliefs is that man is created to accomplish a specific role, within the grand cosmic scheme. According to Egyptian traditions, one cannot succeed in earthly life merely by default. One must use his metaphysical faculty (mind symbolized by the heart) and his physical faculty (action symbolized by the tongue). These actions will be in agreement or at variance with natural harmony. If during his/her earthly life, the actions are not harmonious with nature, s/he will reincarnate again to the earthly realm, to try another time.

The ultimate objective of the earthly man is to develop his/her consciousness to the utmost perfection; it means that he/she becomes harmoniously tuned with nature. This was symbolized in some Egyptian tombs by the deceased soul reciting the **42 Negative Confessions**, on the Judgment Day, before the 42 jurors/**neteru**. [More later in chapter 29.] The successful person was declared to be Sound, by the Grand Jury as **Maa Kheru** — True of Voice.

Since all creation, including human, came as a result of the word (sound), the reunification with our Divine Origin must follow the same route back, i.e. with (true) sound — resonating with NaTuRe (**NeTeRu**).

Go Your Own Way (Ma-at)

The Ancient Egyptian religion is not a matter of creed and dogma, but rather of a personal charter. Each one of us is an individual. As it is shown throughout this book, the Ancient Egyptians implemented their beliefs in individuality in all their texts. As shown earlier, there were never two identical transformational (funerary) or medical (so-called "magical") texts for any two individuals.

One must live his/her own life, and each one of us must go his/her own way, guided by **Ma-at**. The concept of **Ma-at** has permeated all Egyptian writings, from the earliest times and throughout Egyptian history. The concept by which not only men, but also the **neteru** (gods) themselves were governed. **Ma-at** is not easily translated or defined by one word. Basically, we might say that it means *that which, of right, should be; that which is according to the proper order and harmony of the cosmos and of* **neteru** *and men, who are part of it.*

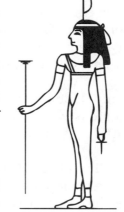

Ma-at could be favorably compared with the Eastern concept of *karma* and the Western concept of *common sense*.

Ma-at, *The Way*, encompasses the virtues, goals, and duties that define the acceptable, if not ideal, social interaction and personal behavior. **Ma-at** is maintained in the world by the correct actions and personal piety of its adherents.

The Egyptians felt that they did not need codifications of **Ma-at** or its related humanistic ethics. Man had a vivid awareness of his/her inner sense of human justice. Additionally, codifications of moral behavior is impractical. For example, to state a commandment, such as "Thou shalt not kill", is not applicable in a case of self-defense. Therefore, the most and only effective way to describe correct actions is with the use of proverbs. An example proverb, such as *One reaps what one sows*, can never be translated into a complete list of commandments. Yet the symbolism of the proverb is easily understood by everyone. It is neither too specific nor too vague.

   The Ancient Egyptian wisdom has always laid great emphasis on the cultivation of ethical behavior and service to society. The constant theme of the Egyptian wisdom literature was the 'acting out' of Truth — **Maa-Kheru** — on earth. The expected conduct and the ideas of responsibility and retribution were expressed in several literary compositions that are usually termed as wisdom texts. Among them are the 30 chapters of **The Teaching of Amenemope**, which contain collections of poetic phrases of moral content and advice.

   The 30 chapters of **The Teaching of Amenemope** were later echoed in the Old Testament's *Book of Proverbs*. Numerous verbal parallels, occur between this Egyptian text and the Bible, such as the opening lines of the first chapter:

Give your ears, listen to the words which are spoken, give your mind to interpreting them. It is profitable to put them in your heart.

   There were additional practical wisdom texts of systematic instructions, composed of maxims and precepts.

   Some of the wisdom proverbs, as collected from survived Egyptian papyri include:

- Don't be proud of earthly goods or riches, for they come

to you from God without your help.
- Don't repeat slanders.
- Deliver messages accurately.
- Be content.
- Be industrious, an idle man is not honorable.
- Do not enter uninvited into the house of another.
- Do not look around in the house of another. If you see anything, be silent about it, and don't relate it to others.
- Speak not too much, for men are deaf to the man of many words.
- Guard your speech, for "a man's ruin lies in his tongue".
- Do not overeat.
- Don't eat bread while another person is present unless you share the bread with him.
- He who is rich this year, may become a pauper next year.
- Be respectful, and do not sit down while another stands who is older than you, or who holds a higher office than yours.

As one charters his/her way through the earthly realm, it is beneficial to get tips from your spiritual guide — the **khu**. Each person has a **khu** — a luminous guardian angel [see page 108]. These luminous spirits are eager to help you see the way, but no one can do it for you. You must do it on your own.

We are not born sinners; we are born with the power of choice. The earthly being must use his cerebral instrument to choose his actions. Each one of us has a heart (consciousness/mind) and a tongue (action/deliverance). Each one of us must know how to manage the energies — all the forces, desires, emotions, etc, in and around us.

How the Egyptians dealt with, for example, sexual desires and egotism, will be described next.

Tame That Bull

The universe cannot exist without the ability to replicate, i.e. reproduce. The wild bull, which is a nearly universal symbol for sexual power, symbolizes boundless strength and fertility. Bulls are esteemed for their sexuality, for a single animal can impregnate an entire herd. As such, the wild bull is a symbol for untamed sexual energy.

Egyptian traditions believe in taming (not denying) the sexual energy. The lassoing and taming of the wild bull symbolizes the control of such energy, as depicted on many Egyptian wall reliefs. Shown below is a wall relief in the temple of **Abtu**, depicting Ramses II and a prince controlling a bull. The symbolic bull is not bullied, injured, or killed. It is not a frivolous game.

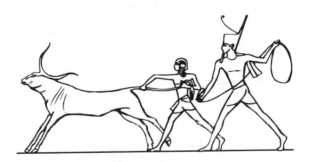

In Ancient and Baladi Egypt, boys are circumcised shortly after reaching puberty, mostly during the *mouleds* (saints' birthday celebrations). After the operation, they live in isolation, where the boys will be actively transformed into adulthood by learning what adults must know to assume societal responsibilities. This will be the metaphysical and physical *boot camp*.

Boys are taught how to manage their inner energies. Teaching the male members of the society self-control is an essential aspect of any society.

Don't Be An Ass

Controlling the ego was/is one of the most important ethical requirements in Ancient and Baladi Egypt.

One of the Egyptian King's title was, *The Most Humble*. His abode while on earth was made of mud-brick, the same material used by the humblest peasants.

The ego is symbolized by the ass. One must know how to control it, by riding the ass — the ego. Egyptian scenes (such as the one shown below) and texts provide the ass

analogy that was resonated later in the following biblical verses, which describe the same concept of being humble and controlling the ego.

> *"Behold, your king is coming to you, humble, and mounted on an ass, and on a colt, the foal of an ass."* *[Matthew, 21:5]*

The Ancient Egyptian transformational (funerary) texts show that one must overcome many obstacles on one's way to the ultimate reunification. One of these obstacles is the ego. To reunite with the Divine we must be ego-free.

The symbolic Ancient Egyptian scene below shows **Heru** (Horus) and his four sons, each armed with a knife, demonstrating to **Ausar** (Osiris) their success in controlling the ego. Their success is symbolized by the ass-headed man (symbol of the ego in man), with knives stuck in his body and bound by his arms to the forked stick.

Be humble. Don't be an ass. In an **Instruction** given in 2380 BCE to a soon-to-be high official, the words begin as follows:

Do not be arrogant because you are learned; do not be over-confident because you are well informed. Consult the ignorant man as well as the wise one.

Chapter 28

Peace With Earth

The Tenants' Rights & Obligations

The Ancient and Baladi Egyptian beliefs in Animism were also reflected in their traditional relationships between people and earth. The Egyptians believed/believe that land had no value apart from people, and, conversely, that people could not exist without land. They recognize and respect the supernatural residents of the land — any land. The spirits of a place (trees, rock outcroppings, rivers, snakes, and other animals and objects) were identified and placated by the original founders, who arrived and inhabited the land at an earlier time. The spirits of the land might vary with each place, or be so closely identified with a group's welfare that they were carried to a new place, as part of the continuity of a group with its former home.

The rights of a group, defined by common genealogical descent, were linked to a particular place and the settlements within it, not through "ownership", but because of their pact with the primordial spirits of the land/site. The spirits, both of family and place, demanded loyalty to communal virtues and to the authority of the elders in maintaining ancient beliefs and practices.

Newcomers (spiritual migrants) join the local spirit population in a new covenant between themselves and the local spirits. This covenant legitimized their arrival. In return for regular homage to these spirits, the founders could claim perpetual access to local resources. In so doing, they became the lineage in charge of the hereditary local priesthood and village headship, and were/are recognized as "tenants of the place" by later human arrivals.

The Ancient Egyptian transformational (funerary) texts maintain the same theme regarding the tenants' rights and obligations. As such, a new spirit must gain the acceptance and support of previous spirits, in each of the realms of the "other world". [More details in chapter 29.]

This spirit of Animism makes people environmentalists, for they treat everything with care and respect. Such coexistence with nature — in all its forms — was a mandatory requirement of each person. Here are a few of the **42 Negative Confessions** that emphasize that one must be true environmentalist in order to succeed in reuniting with the Source.

    7-   I have not plundered the neteru.
    16- I have not laid waste the ploughed land.
    22- I have not polluted myself.
    34- I have not fouled the water.
    36- I have never cursed the neteru.

Neteru means the divine essence (spirits) impuded in everything — plants, air, water, minerals, ...etc.

Such respect for the spirits of the land is indicative of a peaceful (non-invasive) people who will not violate anybody or any land. Egyptians, as such, are very peaceful people. For the Ancient and Baladi Egyptians, stepping on a foreign land in peace or in war, was done with careful consideration to the land and its inhabitants.

Rules of Engagement

Egypt was not interested in an empire, and certainly not in military occupation. Egypt was only interested in neutralizing the hostile elements that threatened to disrupt her own security. There were never Egyptian colonies, and only a handful of foreign wars throughout its long history. After a war ended, they left the foreign land and its people, and returned home.

War, for the Ancient Egyptians, followed rules as strict as a chess game, and had specific rituals. They were truly the civilized people. The wars of the 20th century of bombing and burning would have been considered unthinkable barbaric actions.

The common scene on the outer walls of the temples, and the walls of the outer courtyards, symbolizes the battle of the forces of light, represented by the King (the spiritual or solar principle), subduing the forces of darkness, represented by the foreign enemies. The repetition of this scene at temples throughout Egypt, is purely symbolic, and not a representation of actual historical events.

Part

Going Home

Chapter 29

Life After Earth

The Soul Transmigration

The Egyptians' preoccupation — almost obsession — with the ideas of birth and rebirth was a fundamental element of their funerary beliefs: rebirth was one of the stages of existence in the afterlife. Egyptian texts state clearly that the **"soul is in heaven, the body in the earth"** [Pepi I Tomb], i.e. they never expected the physical body to rise again.

The first known reference to a "second birth" occurs in the CLXXXII[nd] Chapter of the *Book of Coming Forth by Light*, wherein **Ausar** (Osiris) is addressed as,

> *"...he [Ausar] who giveth birth to men and women a second time"*.

"The Egyptians", according to Herodotus, *"were the first to maintain that the soul of man is immortal"*. The doctrine of transmigration is also mentioned by Plutarch, Plato, and other ancient writers as the general belief among the Egyptians, and it was adopted by Pythagoras and his preceptor Pherecydes, as well as other philosophers of Greece.

At the end of one's earthly existence, a performance evaluation will determine which heavenly realm (2-6) a departed soul will reach.

Performance Evaluation

In a book of instructions, an Egyptian King advised his son, the prince, to attain the highest qualities, because upon his death, he would see his whole lifetime in a single instant, and his performance on earth would be reviewed and evaluated by the judges. Even as far back as the period of the 6th Dynasty, we find the idea that heaven was reserved for those who had performed their duty to man and to the Divine Powers while on earth. No exceptions were made to a King or anyone else.

For example, the Pharaoh Unas (2323 BCE), before he was ready to fly from earth into heaven, was not allowed to start unless the **neteru** (who were about to help him) were satisfied as to the reality of his moral worth. They demanded that no man should have uttered a word against him on earth, and that no complaint should have been made against him in heaven before the **neteru** (gods). Accordingly, in the text of Unas we read:

> *"Unas hath not been spoken against on earth before men, he hath not been accused of sin in heaven before the neteru (gods)."*

As stated earlier, Ancient Egyptians expressed their metaphysical beliefs in a story form, like a sacred drama or a *mystery play*. The following are the Egyptians' symbolic representations of the process of the Judgment Day *Mystery Play*.

1 - The soul of the deceased is led to the Hall of Judgment of the Double-**Ma-at**. She is *double* because the scale balances only when there is an equality of opposing forces. **Ma-at's** symbol is the ostrich feather, representing judgment or truth. Her feather is customarily mounted on the scales.

2 -   **Anbu** (Anubis), as opener of the way, guides the soul to the scales and weighs the heart.

1 - **Ma-at**

2 - **Anbu** (Anubis)

3 - **Amam** (Ammit)

4 - **Tehuti** (Thoth)

5 - The deceased

6 - **Heru** (Horus)

7 - **Ausar** (Osiris)

8 - 42 Judges/Assessors

The heart, as a metaphor for conscience, is weighed against the feather of truth, to determine the fate of the deceased.

3 -   The seated Grand Ancestor — **Ausar** (Osiris) — presides in the Hall of Justice. The jury consists of 42 judges/assessors. Each judge has a specific jurisdiction over a specific sin or fault; each wears a feather of truth on his/her head.

4 -   The spirit of the deceased denies committing each sin/fault before its assigned judge, by reciting the **42 Negative Confessions**. These **Negative Confessions** come from *Chapter CXXV* of *The Book of the Coming Forth by Light* (commonly known as *The Book of the Dead*).

The assigned juror/judge will declare his/her acceptance by declaring **Maa-Kheru** (*True of Voice/Action*).

Here is a translation of the **42 Negative Confessions**. Some of them may seem repetitive, but this is caused by the inability to translate the exact intent and meaning of the original language.

1 - I have not done iniquity.
2 - I have not robbed with violence.
3- I have not stolen.
4- I have done no murder; I have done no harm.
5- I have not defrauded offerings.
6- I have not diminished obligations.
7- I have not plundered the neteru.
8- I have not spoken lies.
9- I have not uttered evil words.
10- I have not caused pain.
11- I have not committed fornication.
12- I have not caused shedding of tears.
13- I have not dealt deceitfully.
14- I have not transgressed.
15- I have not acted guilefully.
16- I have not laid waste the ploughed land.
17- I have not been an eavesdropper.
18- I have not set my lips in motion (against any man).
19- I have not been angry and wrathful except for a just cause.
20- I have not defiled the wife of any man.
21- I have not been a man of anger.
22- I have not polluted myself.
23- I have not caused terror.
24- I have not burned with rage.
25- I have not stopped my ears against the words of Right and Truth. (Ma-at)
26- I have not worked grief.
27- I have not acted with insolence.
28- I have not stirred up strife.
29- I have not judged hastily.
30- I have not sought for distinctions.
31- I have not multiplied words exceedingly.

32- I have not done neither harm nor ill.
33- I have not cursed the King. (i.e. violation of laws)
34- I have not fouled the water.
35- I have not spoken scornfully.
36- I have never cursed the neteru.
37- I have not stolen.
38- I have not defrauded the offerings of the neteru.
39- I have not plundered the offerings of the blessed dead.
40- I have not filched the food of the infant.
41- I have not sinned against the neter of my native town.
42- I have not slaughtered with evil intent the cattle of the neter.

5 - Tehuti (Thoth), scribe of the **neteru** (gods), records the verdict, as **Anbu** (Anubis) weighs the heart against the feather of truth. The outcome is either:

   a - If the pans are not balanced, this means that this person lived simply as matter. As a result, **Amam** (Ammit) would eat this heart. **Amam** is a protean crossbreed.
The imperfected soul will be reborn again (reincarnated) in a new physical vehicle (body), in order to provide the soul an opportunity for further development on earth. This cycle of life/death/renewal continues until the soul is perfected, by fulfilling the **42 Negative Confessions**, during his life on earth.

   b - If the two pans are perfectly balanced, **Ausar** gives favorable judgment, and gives his final **Maa-Kheru** (*True of Voice*).

The perfected soul will go through the process of transformation and the subsequent rebirth. The outcome of his/her evaluation will determine which heavenly level (2-6) a person reaches.

Transformational Texts

The object of one and all Ancient Egyptian transformational (funerary) texts was the same, namely, to procure the resurrection and immortality of the persons on whose behalf they were written and recited. Accompanying texts to the deceased varied in content and style. No transformational ("funerary") texts of any two persons were ever the same. These texts were tailored to match each individual's path. We find the same individuality of texts in the so-called "magical" papyri. [See chapter 20.] The Egyptian texts described in detail the stages of the transformation process from man's earthly existence to the different metaphysical realms.

All these themes are treated with a profusion of details in *The Book of Coming Forth By Light* (**Per-em-hru**), wrongly translated and commonly known as *The Egyptian Book of the Dead.* It consists of over one hundred chapters of varying lengths, which are closely related to the *Unas Transformational (Funerary) Texts* at Saqqara. This book is to be found, in its complete form, only on papyrus scrolls that were wrapped in the mummy swathings of the deceased and buried with him.

Other transformational (so-called *funerary* and *religious*) writings are also closely related to the above-mentioned *Unas Transformational Funerary (Pyramid) Texts.* Each text/writing explores the same basic theme, of life/death/rebirth, i.e. transformation of the soul in the region of the Duat after death, from a different angle. Since no two persons are alike, no two transformational texts are alike. These compositions are known as: *The Book of What Is In the Duat* (or Underworld), *The Book of the Gates, The Book of Caverns, The Litany of Ra, The Book of Aker, The Book of Day,* and *The Book of Night.*

Admission To the New Realm

As a result of the performance evaluation, the departed spirits go to various realms — depending on each's achievement level during their earthly existence.

The transformational texts set in motion the process by which the new soul progresses from one realm to another. S/he must meet other requirements and be accepted before proceeding further. To be admitted to a new realm, the dwellers of each realm must find the newcomer qualified and worthy of joining or passing through that realm. The tenants' rights in the spirited world are the same as in the earthly realm. [See chapter 25.]

The newcomer needs both acceptance and assistance of each realm-dweller as s/he ascends higher and higher. So, in the Unas tomb (rubble pyramid) at Saqqara, we find that the inhabitants of the higher realms — **The People of Light** — found Unas (~ 2323 BCE) to be worthy, and thus are accepting and helping him to ascend and to live among them:

> *Utterance 336*
> *The People of Light bore witness for him;*
> *the hail showers of the sky took hold of him.*
> *They let Unas ascend to Ra.*

> *Utterance 377*
> *Your smell comes to Unas, ye neteru (gods),*
> *the smell of Unas comes to you, ye neteru.*
> *May Unas be with you, ye neteru,*
> *may you be together with Unas, ye neteru.*
> *May Unas live with you, ye neteru,*
> *may you live together with Unas, ye neteru.*

After a long series of adventurous journeys, the resurrected soul, justified and regenerated, will attain a place in the retinue of the **neteru** (gods) — the personifications of the cosmic forces — and eventually take part in the unceasing round of activity that permits the universe a continued existence. The Egyptian writing describes it,

> *becomes a star of gold and joins the company of Ra, and sails with him across the sky in his boat of millions of years.*

Part

IIII
IIII

A New Octave

Chapter 30

The End of the Universe
(A New Beginning - Octave)

Scientists tell us that the galaxies are subjected now to mainly two opposing forces: 1) the *expulsion forces*, which cause all galaxies to move away from us, resulting from the effect of the *Big Bang*; and 2) the *gravitational/contractional forces*, which pull the galaxies together.

Scientists tell us, that at a certain point in time in the future, the universe will stop expanding and start getting smaller. The microwave radiation from the *Big Bang* fireball (which is still rushing around) will start squashing down, heat up and change color again, until it becomes visible once more. The sky will become red, and will then turn orange, yellow, white, ... and will end in the *Big Crunch*, i.e. all the matter and all the radiation in the universe will come crashing together, into one unit.

The *Big Crunch* is not the end by itself, for the reunited, crunched universe — *neutron soup* — will have the potential for a new creation, which is called the *Big Bounce*. The universe, as such, has no beginning and will have no end.

Surprisingly, or not surprisingly, the Ancient Egyptian texts, which described the *Big Bang*, have also described, in the usual Egyptian symbolic terms, both the *Big Crunch* and

the *Big Bounce*. In the Egyptian *Coffin Texts, Spell 1130,* we
read:

> *I have placed millions of years*
> *between me and the son of Geb [who is Ausar/Osiris];*
> *then I shall dwell with him [Ausar/Osiris] in one place.*
> *Mounds will be towns. Towns will be mounds.*
>
> *As for any man who knows this spell,*
> *he descends into the entourage of fire,*
> *without there being a flame against him, for all time and*
> *eternity.*

   • **The first passage** indicates that all the matter and
all the energy in the universe will return to one place —
Nun. This is the *Big Crunch*.
   The first passage also indicates that only **Ausar** (Osiris),
as the cyclical aspect of nature, will remain at the end of the
world, signifying the potential for renewal — *The Big Bounce*.
   then I shall dwell with him [Ausar/Osiris] in one place.

   • **The second passage** indicates that the pure in soul,
will rejoin their divine origin, as he/she:

> *descends into the entourage of fire without there being a*
> *flame being against him for all time and eternity.*

**Let Ma-at
guide you back to
The SOURCE**

Glossary

Amen/Amun/Amon - means *Hidden*, for he is everywhere, but you can't see him. He provides the spirit that animates the universe — in whole and in parts. As the creative aspect, he is identified with Ra, as **Amen-Ra**. As the creative urge that manifests itself as universal sexuality, he is **Min-Amun**.

amulet - a charm or ornament containing special powers or symbolic representation.

Animism - The concept that all things in the universe are animated (energized) by life forces. This concurs, scientifically, with the kinetic theory, where each minute particle of any matter is in constant motion, i.e. energized with life forces.

Baladi - the present silent majority of Egyptians that adhere to the Ancient Egyptian traditions, with a thin exterior layer of islam. The christian population of Egypt is an ethnic minority who came as refugees, from Judaea and Syria to the Ptolemaic/Roman-ruled Alexandria. 2,000 years later, they are easily distinguishable in looks and mannerisms from the majority of native Egyptians.

BCE - **B**efore **C**ommon **E**ra. Also noted in other references as BC.

Book of Coming Forth By Light (Per-em-hru) - consists of over one hundred chapters of varying lengths, which are closely related to the *Unas Transformational/ Funerary (so-called Pyramid) Texts* at Saqqara. This book is to be found, in its complete form, only on papyrus scrolls that were wrapped in the mummy swathings of the deceased and buried with him.

Book of the Dead - *see Book of Coming Forth By Light.*

CE - **C**ommon **E**ra. Also noted in other references as AD.

cosmology - The study of the origin, creation, structure, and orderly operation of the universe, as a whole and of its related parts.

Duat/Tuat - The Underworld, where the soul goes through transformation leading to resurrection.

Heb-Sed - Ancient Egyptian festival associated with the rejuvenation of the spiritual and physical powers of the Pharaoh.

Heru - He is the son of **Ausar**(Osiris) and **Auset**(Isis). He is identified with the king during his lifetime. His centers are located in many places, e.g. Behdet in the Delta, and Edfu in Upper Egypt.

Khepri - A symbol for the transformational power of the sun. It is often represented as a beetle within the sun-disk. **Khepri** is **Ra**, in his form of the scarab beetle.

matriarchy - A society/state/organization, whose descent, inheritance, and governance are traced through the females. It is the woman who transmits political rights, and the husband she chooses then acts as her executive agent.

matrilineal - A society whose descent, inheritance, and governance are based on descent through the maternal line.

mouled - The annual "birthday" celebration of a Wali (folk saint) in Ancient and Baladi Egypt.

neter/netert - A divine principle/function/attribute of the One Great God. (Incorrectly translated as *god/goddess*).

papyrus - could mean either: 1) A plant that is used to make a writing surface. 2) *Paper*, as a writing medium. 3) The text written on it, such as *"Leiden Papyrus"*.

Pyramid Texts - A collection of transformational (funerary) literature that was found in the tombs of the 5ᵗʰ and 6ᵗʰ Dynasties (2465-2150 BCE).

scarab - amulet in the form of a black beetle, symbol of transformation. Also see **Khepri**.

stele - (plural: stelae) - stone or wooden slab or column decorated with commemorative inscriptions.

Tet - a symbolic pillar, representing the backbone of **Ausar** (Osiris), the support of creation. It represents the channel through which the divine spirit might rise through matter to rejoin its source.

ushabti - a small figurine, usually of clay, buried with the mummy and charged with performing duties in the afterlife, on behalf of the deceased.

Wali - A saint-type person who the Baladi and Ancient Egyptians respect, visit, and ask favors. Unlike the christian saints, Wali-s are chosen by ordinary people, based on performance. Once the people can see that this person does indeed have the ability to influence supernatural forces, in order to assist those on earth, and as a result fulfills their wishes, then he or she is considered to be a Wali.

Selected Bibliography

Assmann, J. *Agyptische Hymnen Und Gebete* (Leiden Papyrus p. 312-321). Zürich/Münich, 1975.

Budge, Wallis. *Osiris & The Egyptian Resurrection (2 volumes)*. New York, 1973

Egyptian Book of the Dead (The Book of Going Forth by Day), *The Papyrus of Ani*. USA, 1991.

Erman, Adolf. *Life in Ancient Egypt*. New York, 1971.

Gadalla, Moustafa. *Egypt: A Practical Guide*. USA, 1998.

Gadalla, Moustafa. *Exiled Egyptians: The Heart of Africa*. USA, 1999.

Gadalla, Moustafa. *Historical Deception: The Untold Story of Ancient Egypt - Second Edition*. USA, 1999.

Gadalla, Moustafa. *Pyramid Handbook*. USA, 2000.

Gadalla, Moustafa. *Egyptian Harmony, The Visual Music*. USA, 2000.

Herodotus. *The Histories*, tr. A. de Selincourt. New York and Harmondsworth, 1954.

James, T.G.H. *An Introduction to Ancient Egypt*. London, 1979.

Kepler, Johannes. *The Harmony of the World*. Tr. by E. J. Aiton. USA, 1997.

Lambelet, Edouard. *Gods and Goddesses in Ancient Egypt*. Cairo, 1986.

Lane, E.W. *The Manners and Customs of the Modern Egyptians*. London, 1836.

Parkinson, R.B. *Voices From Ancient Egypt, An Anthology of Middle Kingdom Writings*. London, 1991.

Peet, T. Eric. *The Rhind Mathematical Papyrus*. London, 1923.

Piankoff, Alexandre. *The Litany of Re*. New York, 1964.

Piankoff, Alexandre. *Mythological Papyri*. New York, 1957.

Piankoff, Alexandre. *The Pyramid of Unas Texts*. Princeton, NJ, USA, 1968.

Piankoff, Alexandre. *The Shrines of Tut-Ankh-Amon Texts*. New York, 1955.

Piankoff, Alexandre. *The Tomb of Ramesses VI*. New York, 1954.

Plutarch. *Plutarch's Moralia, Volume V*. Tr. by Frank Cole Babbitt. London, 1927.

Siculus, Diodorus. *Vol 1*. Tr. by C.H. Oldfather. London.

West, John A. *The Travelers Key to Ancient Egypt*. New York, 1989.

Wilkinson, Richard H. *Reading Egyptian Art*. New York, 1994.

Wilkinson, Sir J. Gardner. *The Ancient Egyptians, Their Life and Customs*. London, 1988.

————. *Wings of the Falcon, Life and Thought of Ancient Egypt*, tr. Joseph Kaster. USA, 1968.

Numerous references written in Arabic.

Sources and Notes

I believe that a scholar should not be content with referring to just a single/few references to support a point. A single reference may (and often does) intentionally/unintentionally omit something, or color it. Therefore, several sources must be considered and evaluated, and pieces of evidence must be put together like pieces of a puzzle, in the right location and time.

Listed references in the previous section, **Selected Bibliography** are only referred to for the facts, events, and dates; not for their interpretations of such information.

The absence of several references in the Selected Bibliography does not mean that the author is unfamiliar with them. It only means that in spite of their popularity, they were not found to be credible sources.

Please note: 1) Sources listed are the *primary* sources. Other references in the Selected Bibliography are *secondary* sources; 2) If a reference to a particular Ancient Egyptian text is used in more than one chapter, I will mention it in the first instance only.

It should be noted that Alexandre Piankoff died suddenly, while all his listed books were in progress. As a result, the books are a mix of Piankoff's writing and many others who hold the typical dogmatic academic conteptuous attitude. The statements quoted in the preface of this book are Piankoff's, who had a great respect for the spiritual depth of the Ancient Egyptian text. Unfortunately, most of the text in his books was written by others. One must notice the marked difference in the writing.

Chapter 1

Cosmic Consciousness - All references, even if most references call it "superstition", which still means cosmic consciousness.
Monotheism - Budge, West, Piankoff (*Ra*), Kaster.
Mystery Plays - Plutarch, Gadalla (*Egyptian Cosmology, 1ˢᵗ ed, Egyptian Harmony*), Kaster.

Chapter 2

All references, but especially Plutarch, Gadalla (*Historical Deception*), West.

Chapter 3

Piankoff (*Tut*), Kaster, Gadalla (*Egyptian Harmony, Historical Deception*), Peet (*Rhind Mathematical Papyrus*), Plutarch, Assmann (*Leiden Papyrus*).

Chapter 4

Pyramid Texts - Piankoff (*Unas*).
Bremner-Rhind Papyrus, Piankoff (*Shrines of Tut*), and Kaster.

Chapter 5

Practically all references.

Bremner-Rhind Papyrus - Piankoff, West, Kaster.
Neheb-Kau - Kaster, Lambelet, Gadalla (*Egyptian Harmony*).
Twin-gendered - Budge, Piankoff (*Unas*), Gadalla (being an Egyptian native), and numerous books in Arabic.
Ra and Ausar - Piankoff (all references), Budge.
Book of Coming Forth By Light, Chapter 17, Piankoff and *Papyrus of Ani.*
Set and Heru - Practically all references.
Heru and Tehuti - Shabaka Stele (*Piankoff - Ra*), Kaster, Gadalla (*Egyptian Harmony*).

Chapter 6

Practically all references, especially Plutarch, Gadalla (*Egyptian Harmony*).

Chapter 7

Practically all references.
Four Elements - Plutarch.
Leiden Papyrus - Assmann.
Tet Pillar - Budge.

Chapter 8

Plutarch, Gadalla (*Egyptian Harmony*).

Chapter 9

Assmann (*Leiden Papyrus*), Gadalla (*Egyptian Harmony*), West.

Chapter 10

Budge, Piankoff (all references), Gadalla (*Historical Deception, Egyptian Harmony*).

Chapter 11

Leiden Papyrus - Assmann.
Coffin Texts - Parkinson.
Other Items - Gadalla (*Egyptian Harmony*), practically all references.

Chapter 12

Animistic beliefs and practices - Budge, Gadalla (being a native Egyptian).
The Nine Realms - Piankoff (*Unas*), Gadalla (being a native Egyptian), numerous books in Arabic.

Chapter 13

West, Budge, Piankoff, Gadalla (*Historical Deception, Egyptian Harmony*).

Chapter 14

Ra & Grand Ennead - Piankoff (*Re*), Assmann (*Leiden Papyrus, Herodotus*), Gadalla (*Egypt: A Practical Guide*).
Scarab Symbolism - text of Horapollo Niliaeus - Piankoff (*Ramses*).

Chapter 15

Book of the Dead - (*Papyrus of Ani*).
Ra and Tehuti - Gadalla (*Egyptian Harmony*), Peet.
Name Calling - Book of Divine Cow - Piankoff (*Tut*).
Ra and Auset - Kaster, Erman.
Harmony of Spheres - Gadalla (*Egyptian Harmony*), Diodorus, West.
All other points - practically all references, especially Kaster, Gadalla (all references).

Chapter 16

West, Gadalla (*Exiled Egyptians*).

Chapter 17

Budge, Gadalla (*Exiled Egyptians, Historical Deception*), West, Piankoff (all references).

Chapter 18

Gadalla (*Egyptian Cosmology, 1ˢᵗ edition*), West, Parkinson [re: the astronomical record-keeping of **Sabt** (Sirius) Star].

Chapter 19

Gadalla (*Historical Deception, Egyptian Cosmology, 1ˢᵗ ed*), West, Plutarch.

Chapter 20

Divinized human parts - Painkoff (*Re, Unas*), Papyrus of Ani.

The Big Bang Mystery Play - Kaster, Piankoff (*Unas, Bremner-Rhind Papyrus*).

Astrological Maps - Piankoff (*Re*), Gadalla (*Egyptian Cosmology, 1ˢᵗ ed, Historical Deception*).

Hand of God - R.H. Wilkinson.

Metaphysical Parts - Piankoff (*Re*), Ani Papyrus, Kaster, Gadalla (*Egyptian Cosmology, 1ˢᵗ ed*).

Human Units - Gadalla (*Egyptian Harmony*).

Chapter 21

Budge, Gadalla (*Egyptian Cosmology, 1ˢᵗ ed*, being a native Egyptian), West.

Chapter 22

Herodotus, Gadalla (*Exiled Egyptians*), Budge.

Chapter 23

Gadalla (*Exiled Egyptians, Historical Deception*), Diodorus, Herodotus.

Chapter 24

Budge, Gadalla (*Historical Deception, Exiled Egyptians*).

Chapter 25

Budge, Gadalla (*Exiled Egyptians,* and being a native Egyptian).

Chapter 26

Gadalla (*Egyptian Cosmology, 1st ed, Historical Deception, Egyptian Harmony*).

Chapter 27

Sound Reunification - practically all references.

Your Own Way - Kaster, Gadalla (*Egyptian Cosmology, 1st ed, Historical Deception*), Budge, Piankoff.
Tame That Bull - Gadalla (*Exiled Egyptians*).
Don't Be An Ass - Budge, Gadalla (*Historical Deception*).

Chapter 28

Tenants' Rights - Gadalla (*Exiled Egyptians*, and being a native Egyptian).
Rules of Engagement - West, Gadalla (*Historical Deception*).

Chapter 29

Soul Transmigration - Herodotus, Budge, Piankoff.
Performance Evaluation - Practically all references.
Transformational Texts - Gadalla (*Historical Deception*), West, Piankoff (*Unas*).
Individualized transformational texts - see Piankoff (*Mythological Papyri*) which contains 30 different texts with no two tombs are alike.
Admission to New Realm - Budge, Piankoff (*Unas*).

Chapter 30

Coffin Texts - Parkinson.

Index

Tehuti Research Foundation

Tehuti Research Foundation (T.R.F.) is a non-profit, international organization, dedicated to Ancient Egyptian studies. Our books are engaging, factual, well researched, practical, interesting, and appealing to the general public.

The books listed below are authored by T.R.F. chairman, Moustafa Gadalla.

Visit our website at:
http://www.egypt-tehuti.org
E-mail address: info@egypt-tehuti.org

About Our Books

Egyptian Harmony: The Visual Music
ISBN: 0-9652509-8-9 (pbk.), 192 pages, US$11.95

This book reveals the Ancient Egyptian incredible and comprehensive knowledge of harmonic proportion, sacred geometry, music, and number mysticism, as manifested in their texts, temples, tombs, ...etc., throughout their known history. Discover how the Word (sound) that created the World (forms) was likewise transformed to visual music by the Egyptians into hieroglyphs, art, and architecture. The book surveys the Ancient Egyptian harmonic proportional application in all aspects of their civilization.

Historical Deception
The Untold Story of Ancient Egypt - Second Edition
ISBN: 0-9652509-2-X (pbk.), 352 pages, US$19.95

This book reveals the ingrained prejudices against ancient Egypt, from both the religious groups, who deny that

Egypt is the source of their creed, and Western rationalists, who deny the existence of science and philosophy prior to the Greeks. The book contains 46 chapters, with many interesting topics, such as the Egyptian medical knowledge about determining the sex of the unborn, and much, much more.

Exiled Egyptians: The Heart of Africa
ISBN: 0-9652509-6-2 (pbk.), 352 pages, US$19.95

Read about the forgotten Ancient Egyptians, who fled the foreign invasions and religious oppressions, and rebuilt the ancient Egyptian model system in Africa, when Egypt itself became an Arab colony. Find out how a thousand years of islamic jihads have fragmented and dispersed the African continent into endless misery and chaos. Discover the true causes and dynamics of the history of African slavery. Understand the genius of the ancient Egyptian/African religious, social, economical, and political systems.

Pyramid Handbook - Second Edition
ISBN: 0-9652509-4-6 (pbk.), 192 pages, US$11.95

A complete handbook about the pyramids of Ancient Egypt during the Pyramid Age. It contains: the locations and dimensions of interiors and exteriors of the pyramids; the history and builders of the pyramids; theories of construction; theories on their purpose and function, the sacred geometry that was incorporated into the design of the pyramids; and much, much more.

Tut-Ankh-Amen: The Living Image of the Lord
ISBN: 0-9652509-9-7 (pbk.), 144 pages, US$9.50

This book provides the overwhelming evidence from archeology, the Dead Sea Scrolls, the Talmud, and the Bible itself, that Tut-Ankh-Amen was the historical character of Jesus. The book examines the details of Tut's birth, life, death, resurrection, family roots, religion, teachings, etc., which were duplicated in the biblical account of Jesus. The book also reveals the world's greatest conspiracy and cover-up, which re-created the character of Jesus, living in another time (Roman era) and another place (Palestine/Israel).

Egypt: A Practical Guide
ISBN: 0-9652509-3-0 (pbk.), 256 pages, US$8.50

A no-nonsense, no-clutter, practical guide to Egypt, written by an Egyptian-American Egyptologist. Quick, easy, and comprehensive reference to sites of antiquities and recreation. Find your way with numerous maps and illustrations. Tips are included to help understanding both the modern and Ancient Egyptian cultures. This pocket-sized book is informative, detailed, and contains an illustrated glossary.

Tehuti Research Foundation

Ordering Information

Name_____

Address_____

City_____

State/Province_____

Country _____Tel. (_____) _____

_____ Books @ $11.95 (Egyptian Cosmology)   = $
_____ Books @ $11.95 (Egyptian Harmony)   = $
_____ Books @ $19.95 (Historical Deception)   = $
_____ Books @ $11.95 (Pyramid Handbook)   = $
_____ Books @ $ 9.50 (Tut-Ankh-Amen)   = $
_____ Books @ $ 8.50 (Egypt: Practical Guide)   = $
_____ Books @ $19.95 (Exiled Egyptians)   = $_____
                Subtotal   = $

North Carolina residents, add 6 % Sales Tax   = $
Shipping: (N. America only) $2.00 for 1ˢᵗ book   = $
     for each additional book $1 x _____   = $
Outside N. Amer. (per weight/destination)   = $_____
                 Total   = $

Payment: [ ] Check (payable: Tehuti Research Foundation)
          [ ] Visa [ ] MasterCard [ ] Discover

Card Number: _____

Name on Card: _____ Exp. Date: ___/___

Tehuti Research Foundation
P.O. Box 39406
Greensboro, NC   27438-9406   U.S.A.
Call TOLL FREE (North America) and order now   888-826-7021
Or FAX your order   212-656-1460
e-mail: info@egypt-tehuti.org